MR GRAND NATIONAL

MR GRAND NATIONAL

The Story of Fred Winter

Jockey and Trainer

by DAVID HEDGES

PELHAM BOOKS

First published in Great Britain by
PELHAM BOOKS LTD
26 Bloomsbury Street
London, W.C.1
1969

© 1969 *by David Hedges and Fred Winter*

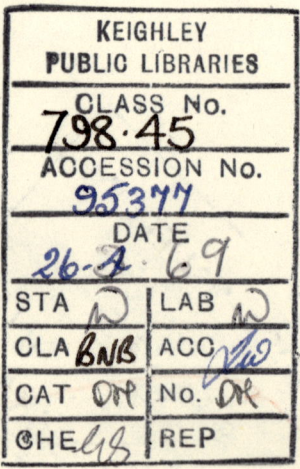
7207 0193 7

Set and printed in Great Britain by
Tonbridge Printers Ltd, Peach Hall Works, Tonbridge, Kent
in Baskerville eleven on thirteen point, and bound by
James Burn at Esher, Surrey

CONTENTS

CONTENTS

ILLUSTRATIONS

INTRODUCTION

In my opinion, Fred Winter is the greatest jockey ever to have ridden under National Hunt Rules, and it has been a privilege to write his story – as far as it goes.

He rode two Grand National winners and already as a trainer, he has saddled the winners of two Grand Nationals, and it is certain that he will continue to make headlines, as he has done ever since he first become involved in racing.

In expressing my thanks to Ryan Price, to John Lawrence, and many others who have helped me with facts and information for this book, I would particularly like to mention Fred's brother, John Winter, who was really his first chronicler.

A serious illness prevented John from following his own career as a jockey, but he maintained a devoted record in scrap books and ledgers of Fred's successes. The five heavy scrap books filled with cuttings covering every aspect of Fred's career, and the book in which John entered every ride which Fred ever had have been an enormous help to me.

The note which John wrote at the end of the final scrap book, after Fred had retired from riding, speaks for itself :

'Fred retires in the knowledge that to all he has always given of his best. No man can do more. In all stories there are untold tales – the times of adversity when all looked lost, the falls, the injuries and the courageous fight back to the top, the knowledge that there is always someone ready to take your place.

'Fred overcame all this in his long and distinguished career. He has been a tremendous example to me personally, and his courage has been an example which has helped me to overcome my own adversities. I cannot think of there ever being a greater jockey or a finer person. I am very proud indeed to be his brother.'

D.H.

CHAPTER ONE

A PAINFULLY ACQUIRED ART

'No, no, put it down, put down that whip.' The words of Fred Winter were lost among the uproar from the crowd as the Grand National leaders battled up that most daunting stretch of ground on any racecourse, the 494 yards from the last fence at Aintree to the winning post.

With almost a quarter of a mile to go the American horse, Jay Trump, was showing signs of resentment. His rider, Tommy Smith, flourished the whip to draw a last effort out of his tiring mount, as he and the favourite Freddie fought it out, many lengths clear of anything else.

'For God's sake put it down,' shouted Fred amidst the turmoil on top of the County Stand, and, as if he heard him, Tommy Smith put down his whip and rode Jay Trump with his hands and heels.

The big horse stopped twitching his tail in protest, lowered his head again and ran on to hold off Freddie's challenge by three-quarters of a length – the first horse to win the two toughest prizes in American and English steeple-chasing, the Maryland Hunt Cup and the Grand National.

'What about that,' said Fred Winter with a huge grin, turning to the two women with him, his wife Diana and Frances Smith, wife of the now exhausted and elated rider of Jay Trump. 'How about that.'

Behind the stands, Aintree erupted again as Tommy and Jay Trump, now escorted by mounted police, ploughed their way back through the crowd to the unsaddling enclosure. Fred, Diana and Frances fought their own route to the same place through a crowd strongly laced with ecstatic Americans.

The television cameras came in close on the scene as the owner, Mrs Mary Stephenson, kissed Jay Trump, embraced Fred and Tommy. Two policemen escorted Tommy through a seething crowd to the weighing room, and back to the unsaddling enclosure to be interviewed by the B.B.C's David Coleman.

Then to the press room, for a grilling more suitable for a sharp-witted politician than a man who was still finding his breath after riding four miles and 856 yards over 30 huge fences and had landed for Mrs Stephenson the £22,000 prize that they had made their target nine months earlier.

It had been Fred Winter who had stood on the table in the press room three years earlier to answer the questions after he had won the National on Kilmore, and five years before that too when the massive Sundew had given him his first victory over Europe's sternest steeplechase course.

But this time, in 1965, Fred had to ride the race from the stands. The man who had thrilled millions of racegoers with his own brave exploits in this maddest of all ways of earning a living, was now the trainer instead of the jockey – trainer of both the horse and the jockey.

He had spent hours discussing tactics with Tommy Smith, passed on everything he knew of the painfully acquired art of riding over Aintree's fences: what to do, where to be at any given moment in the race, the route to follow.

He had given Tommy a leg up in the paddock, looked up at him with a smile, said 'Have a good time, God bless', and gone to the top of the stands with a quiet prayer that everything that had passed between them would bear fruit in the shape of victory.

And it worked. The months of planning, talking, worrying about infection from the coughing epidemic which had swept through the country, ended in a win in the Grand National which showed that not only could Fred Winter ride National winners but that he could train them as well, and he had the ability, uncommon in great practitioners, to pass his knowledge, his confidence and a spark of his own ability on to other people.

Twelve months after he had sent Tommy Smith and Jay Trump out to win the Grand National, he did exactly the same with Tim Norman and Anglo. The Winter story which had commanded attention ever since he had ridden his first winner as a 13-year-old boy weighing 5 st 12 lb was launched on another successful phase.

Yet it could all so easily have ended when Fred broke his back in only his seventh ride over jumps.

CHAPTER TWO

ONE WINTER WILL REMEMBER
THIS SUMMER

As far back as Fred can remember, he was going to be a jockey. He was steeped in racing from the day he was born. His mother came from an Irish farming family called Flanagan. They farmed at Dolphins Barn, now swallowed up in the suburbs of Dublin.

An aunt of hers was married to politician Willie Cosgrove, Ireland's first President, but her two sisters, Sheila and May, were both wed to jockeys – one to Morny Wing, one of Ireland's best flat race jockeys, and the other to Billy Smith, who broke his neck in a fall at Gatwick.

Fred's mother, who now lives with her other trainer son, John Winter, at Newmarket, herself married a jockey, Fred Winter, senior. He was a first-class rider before the First World War and rode 76 winners in a season when he was only 16, finishing fourth in the list of jockeys when he was still an apprentice. He was just 16 years old when he won the Oaks in 1911 on Cherimoya, a filly who had never been on a racecourse in her life before and never ran again as she broke down.

It was the only classic that Fred, senior, did win, largely because he spent the whole of the war in Germany in the Ruhleben prisoner of war camp. He had been engaged to ride for the German National Stud, which he was doing with great success when war broke out. Officials sportingly gave him 24 hours to get out of the country but he could not make it and was interned. When he went to Germany he was

14

riding at the ideal weight of 7 st 5 lb and when he returned after four years of inactivity he weighed 11 stone.

He rode for a few seasons over hurdles and got his weight down sufficiently to have rides again on the flat, but it was never the same again. Those who saw him ride in flat races rated him as top class, a strong finisher, and a man who could hand it out during a race if anyone was unwise enough to try anything on.

It was in a bungalow called Cherimoya at Andover that Fred Winter, junior, was born on September 20, 1926. His father was then first jockey to Frank Hartigan's stable. Later the family moved to Newmarket, where Fred, senior, rode for the Joel family for two years until he retired in 1929. The Winters then went to live at Bredenbury, a house and stables near Epsom Downs railway station.

There is a photograph in a tailor's shop in Epsom High Street of Fred at the age of four and a half leading out a towering racehorse. At this age, too, he could be seen riding a grey pony in canters on the Downs alongside his father. Fred weighed three stone.

He had two elder sisters Sheila and Pat and a younger brother John, and all were proficient in the saddle. Pat is now married to recently retired flat race jockey Doug Smith, and John, whose highly promising career as a jockey was ended by a serious illness, is doing well as a trainer at Newmarket.

Living in Epsom when Fred was growing up were the Dicks, and Dave Dick, that mad, brave, effervescent character whose enforced retirement from National Hunt riding in 1965 following a schooling accident took some of the fun out of the game for many people, was Fred's inseparable boyhood companion. They both learned to ride on the same pony, and went to school together at Ewell Castle.

Fred often stayed with the Dicks during school holidays, when he and Dave usually managed to contrive ways of living dangerously. Fred recalls climbing over the walls of the mental asylum opposite the Dicks' home, and hiding

15

behind the bushes to watch the inmates. Dropping back to safety afterwards they probably experienced the same sense of relief that they felt years later when safely negotiating the last fence in a novices' steeplechase.

At an early age Fred was competing in gymkhanas and horse shows and he won many prizes. He was schooled by that past-master of the production of young show jumpers, both human and equine, George Hobbs.

In 1939, at the age of 13, he shared first place with three others in a jumping class at Richmond Royal Horse Show on a pony of George Hobbs' called Mickey (he was still going strong in 1956 at the age of 33). One of the others in first place was ridden by Miss Pat Smythe, and the field included many who went on to fame in the show ring, among them Douglas Bunn and Peter Robeson.

It was in racing that Fred's heart lay. By this time he was riding out every morning with his father's team, when school did not interfere, and when he was 13 he was schooling horses over hurdles. In that year his father obtained permission from the headmaster at Ewell Castle for Fred to have a day off from school to ride in a flat race at Newbury.

His father drove him to Newbury, and his mother and brother John went too. His mount was Mr Winter's two-year-old Tam o' Shanter in the Lambourn Nursery over six furlongs, and his father took him into the jockeys' room and put him in the care of valet Ernie Hales who had looked after Fred, senior, during his own riding career.

However apprehensive Fred may have felt about this first appearance in public, he did not show it. A Press Association report said 'Chewing gum, he mounted and cantered to the post with the confidence of an old hand. He got well away from the gate, finished ninth, and was cheered at the end of the race'.

Another writer said, 'It's my job in this column to find you winners – well for a change, I will select a jockey who has yet to ride his first winner – his name is Fred Winter and

16

I predict a brilliant career for this coming champ.'

The fact that Fred was the son of a former top class jockey no doubt had a lot to do with the amount of publicity his first ride attracted, and the man who made the forecast of a brilliant career on the basis of having seen Fred finish ninth in a field of 21 was somewhat bold. There is just one point about this. He was absolutely right.

After only a few more rides, Fred seized his chance in May, 1940, in a £100 race at Salisbury and rode his first winner. He drove Tam o' Shanter home with hands and heels to win by a length and a half from Jeepers Creepers, ridden by Tommy Lowrey.

The other jockeys who rode in the race included Harry Wragg, Gordon Richards, Eph Smith and Michael Beary. Fred, weighing only 5 st 12 lb, and with nearly three stone of lead in the weight cloth, lugged his saddle back to the scales with a wide smile on his face, amidst congratulations from the other jockeys, several of whom had ridden against his father 20 years earlier.

His win earned him the accolade for 'The Week's Best Performance' in *The Racehorse*, and also what was probably the first example in a newspaper of a Winter pun: 'One Winter at least will remember this summer'.

A fortnight later Fred won again on Tam o' Shanter, this time by only three-quarters of a length from the well backed Mythical Maid, trained by Staff Ingham. It was an apprentices' race so the opposition in terms of jockeyship was not so strong as it had been at Salisbury, but Fred again impressed watchers by his style.

His flat racing career was well and truly launched, and Fred Winter, senior, decided that, as he did not have many horses himself, it would help Fred if he was apprenticed to someone with a larger stable and more opportunity of giving him rides. His indentures were transferred to a friend of the family, Henri Jelliss, who had been a riding contemporary of Fred Winter, senior, and was now training in Newmarket.

17

Fred went into lodgings in Newmarket but this phase of his career was not a success. Fred had some 80 rides during 1941, and had only two wins, one at Newmarket on Jeepers Creepers, the horse he had defeated on the occasion of his first victory at Salisbury, and the other on Hey Presto in an apprentices' race at Haydock Park. But, somehow, Fred was not taking his riding career very seriously. The war was in full swing, overshadowing everything, there was little racing, and with prospects not appearing bright, he did not seem to have any sense of ambition at this stage.

By the end of the year his weight was going up by leaps and bounds, and he started 1942 weighing nearly 8 st 7 lb. It was obvious that his days in flat racing were limited. His father had moved to Southfleet in Kent to train privately for Mr Percy Bartholomew, and Fred rejoined him there, working as a stable lad, but the stable had few horses and Fred was not really needed.

He was keen on joining the R.A.F. and had gone into the Air Training Corps, but at this stage he was too young for the Air Force. So, with the idea of acquiring some practical knowledge of planes, he went into a factory at Feltham where damaged planes were repaired. Fred missed being with horses and riding out each morning.

He did go back into racing for nine months, working as a stable lad at Epsom for Walter Nightingall, before he finally joined not the R.A.F. but the Army.

He had passed for aircrew, but was warned that, now the war had taken a turn for the better, there was little chance of flying, so he switched to the Army and, as he puts it, 'fell for the sales talk of a fellow with a red beret and a dagger in his belt' who came round looking for volunteers for the Parachute Regiment. The beauty of it was that Fred got half a crown a day extra, which was a lot of money in those days at the age of 18.

Fred found parachuting a great thrill at first, and enjoyed the training with eight jumps. After qualifying as a parachutist, he achieved a commission in the West Kents. It was 18 months before he was required to jump out of an aeroplane again, and by that time he found the experience much less attractive. Fred was drafted to Palestine for nine months, but the war was virtually over.

His demobilisation did not come until 1948, and he had plenty of time to think about what he was going to do when he left the Army. At first glance, he did not fancy his prospects a great deal. His weight ruled him out for the job that he had been trained for, flat racing, and the training that the Army had given him so far did not qualify him for earning a living in any particular way in civilian life.

Sitting in the officers' mess in Palestine reading an illustrated magazine, he saw a photograph of horses jumping in a race, and it struck him that there was not much he could do in life except ride horses, and that he should try his hand at National Hunt racing.

Fred wrote to his father, who had always kept a few jumpers as well as flat horses, and asked him if he would give him a chance to ride over jumps when he came out of the Army. The reply was 'yes' and on a day in December, 1947, he went home to Southfleet on demobilisation leave.

A 12-year-old called Carton, who knew a good deal more about the jumping game than did Fred, was his first schoolmaster. He rode Carton over three fences in the paddock at Southfleet to see how he went, and on the strength of this, and a certain amount of ability that he had shown as a flat race rider, Fred approached a family friend, Mr Brian Garrood, who had horses in training with John Goldsmith, and asked if he could ride his four-year-old Bambino II at Kempton Park on Boxing Day.

Mr Garrood agreed, but he must have regretted it when he saw Bambino II go straight to the front and make the running at a strong pace. It was not physical weakness in the saddle that caused this but complete inexperience on Fred's part of the pace at which a two miles' hurdle race should be run. By halfway, Bambino II was exhausted and he dropped back to finish fifth. It was not an auspicious start.

The next day Fred was to ride Carton in a two miles' 'chase, and his father told him exactly what to do. He was to wait with the utmost patience and on no account to make his challenge until the last fence. Fred, now feeling extremely nervous, rode out of the Kempton Park paddock determined at least to do what he was told.

He was riding with his stirrup leathers much too short for a steeplechase, and had very little control of the situation. Fortunately he did not need to, for old Carton jumped faultlessly, drew up to the leaders at the last fence, and then flew home on the flat to win by six lengths. Fred's jumping career was under way.

Commented the *Sporting Chronicle* 'Lieut. Winter is shortly to be demobilised and he will be a welcome addition to our ranks of N.H. riders. He has obviously inherited much of his father's skill, and I cannot remember seeing a jockey who shaped better in his first race over a country.' It was more fulsome praise than Fred thought he was entitled to, but it was a good start.

Carton had played an important part in the lives of both Dave Dick and the Winter family. Fred Winter, senior, had saddled him to win a two-year-old selling race in 1938, he was Dave Dick's first winner on the flat (the lanky giant of today weighed 6 st 5 lb then), as well as Fred's first jumping winner, and between those two events there were eight years.

Carton went on winning races till he was 15 and then went to George Archibald at Newmarket as the trainer's hack. He hated being turned out doing nothing, and, rather than let him linger on miserably after he became too old for further active service, it was decided to put him down at the age of 18.

There had been an enthusiastic reception for Lieut. Winter

as he returned to the Kempton Park unsaddling enclosure on Carton. The Christmas holiday crowd cheered Fred, and back in the jockeys' room, Epsom riders Johnny Gilbert and Ken Mullins, the only faces he had recognised when he stepped into this new field the day before, congratulated him.

Not long after, Fred had his first look at the other side of the coin. He fell when riding Carton's half brother Bright Boy at Kempton Park. It was only his fifth ride :

It was the first real pain I had ever had in my life. We fell at the last but one when I was lying second, and the thought of the three horses behind coming over the fence and landing on top of me absolutely terrified me. I got up and dived for the rails and rolled underneath them before the others arrived. When I got up I felt a bit shaken and my shoulder was very sore. In fact it was dislocated. One of the press men, Fairchild, who used to collect the runners and riders for the papers, always used to pull my leg after that, because he swore it wasn't the fall that dislocated my shoulder but the way I dived under the rails.

This fall put Fred out of action for exactly a month and then he returned to Kempton Park to ride his old friend Carton in a two mile 'chase which brought out Lamento, a brilliant but somewhat unreliable French-bred trained by Peter Cazalet, as well as the consistent Chaka, ridden by Ron Smyth. Fred's orders were again to wait till the last fence.

Chaka fell at the fifth fence leaving Bryan Marshall a long way in front on Lamento, who hit the seventh fence from home hard and from that moment refused to battle. Fred still waited to the last, let out a reef on Carton, and beat Bryan Marshall a neck, which was not a bad thing to do for a jockey struggling to make his name, even if Marshall (who was to finish that season as champion jockey) was not getting much co-operation from his own mount.

21

Fred finished the season with a record of nine rides and two wins. Most of his mounts had been for people who knew him. He had got to know few people outside his father's stable, and he realised that he had a long way to go if he was going to make any progress in a tough and highly competitive sport.

He had a lesson in how tough it could be in his first ride the following season. Once again it was on old Carton, this time on the trappy little course at Folkestone, and orders were the same – wait till the last.

Fred came into the final jump with two horses in front of him, Loyal Monarch and Loyal King. Both were owned by Miss Dorothy Paget, who would sometimes win five or six races at a Folkestone meeting. Champion jockey Bryan Marshall was on Loyal Monarch and as Fred landed over the last fence a length or so behind and was just unleashing Carton's turn of speed to go through on the rails, Bryan looked over and saw him coming.

He shouted 'Look out, look out,' to Paddy Conlon on the stable companion. The latter swung across in an attempt to close the gap, but Carton squeezed through and won half a length and a neck from the two Paget horses. No one on the stands seems to have noticed this drama but the riders behind, who included Lord Mildmay and Bob Turnell, were probably amused to see what was going on.

It was a lesson to Fred. It taught him to keep his eyes open the whole time and to look out for potential trouble :

The secret of taking chances is to have sufficient up your sleeve to get away with it. Many times, people have tried to come up on my inside without having enough speed to get away with it. You have got to know what you have got under you. It's the same as driving a car. If you haven't got sufficient up your sleeve, don't try it.

Seven days after this third taste of victory, Fred broke his back.

CHAPTER THREE

'WHAT THE HELL IS WRONG WITH YOU, WINTER?'

'I don't really know why I didn't pack it up there and then,' said Fred years later, thinking back to the painful months which followed the moment when he fractured his spine as an animal with the appalling name of Tugboat Minnie fell with him in a novices' hurdle at Wye.

He was just setting out on his career. She was 11 years old and had never won a race or even been placed. She started at 20 to 1 and she barely made an effort to jump the first hurdle.

A few minutes later Fred was being carried off to the ambulance room on a stretcher. The comings and goings of the doctors and nurses were watched by an anxious father and mother. Eventually Fred convinced the doctor that he was well enough to go home but in the car he began to feel sharp pains under his armpit.

He went to bed early and the next day laughing or breathing deeply was agony. An X-ray at the local hospital showed nothing, but four days later Fred was still feeling daggers driven into him every time he exerted himself.

A visitor for Sunday lunch at the Winters' home that week-end was Dr Aiden Redmond, who had known the family for many years. He told Fred to lie on a bed, tapped him on the heels and noted the resulting pain, checked him over thoroughly, and sent him to London for another X-ray. It showed that he had two fractured vertebrae.

It was 12 months before Fred rode again.

I honestly don't know why I didn't turn it in. Perhaps I

*had to prove to myself that I had the guts to go on. It
certainly wasn't for love of steeplechasing. I had had two falls
in 12 rides – one which resulted in a dislocated shoulder
which hurt, and the other a broken back, which hurt like
hell. I loved winning races, and I always have done, but the
actual jumping side of it never really appealed to me the
way it seems it does to some people. The jumps have always
been just obstacles in the way between you and winning a
race. Obviously you get a kick out of going to the last and
getting a horse to pick up and gain half a length – that's
quite a thrill – but fences are just in the way to be got over
as best you can with the ultimate objective of passing the
post in front. At the time of that fall, I had won only three
races and quite honestly I was not all that enamoured of the
sport.*

Fred now faced a long convalescence. He had come out of
the Army with little more than his £50 gratuity and a free
suit. The first car he bought when he started riding was a
Ford 8 which had already covered more than 100,000 miles.
He was fortunate that he could live at home with his parents
at Southfleet.

As he grew stronger the daily routine of the stable went
on around him and eventually he was able to ride out and get
his muscles working again.

Staying at Newmarket with his sister Pat and her husband
Doug Smith, Fred went to a dance at the Bedford Lodge
Hotel and met George Archibald, a friend since boyhood
and now training at flat racing's headquarters. George's team
included a few jumpers but Fred was too diffident to ask if
there was any chance of riding any of them, in view of his
record to date.

George himself asked if he was going to start riding again
and added that if Fred liked to come up to Newmarket to do
a bit of schooling, he would give him some rides in races.

Fred drove to Newmarket a few mornings later, and with

every mile he drew nearer, the hollower became the feeling in his stomach. He was not at all convinced that he was doing the right thing in resuming the battle in a sport in which he had got off to such a bad start. 'What the hell do I do if I don't do this?' was the strongest argument that kept him going.

His first effort schooling hurdlers at Newmarket was fortunately not observed by the work watchers who report the gallops on Newmarket Heath for the newspapers.

While strings of horses on the sacred turf nearby went about their work at generally well regulated paces, Fred and two other riders on three young horses set off at sprinting pace over three hurdles, getting the job over just as fast as they could and leaving a trail of flattened hurdles.

There was a loud explosion from the trainer when they rode back. His view was that they were stark raving mad, should never again be allowed on Newmarket Heath and how the hell did they expect horses to learn to jump that way.

He then set about showing them the right way to do it, slowly at first so that the horses learned to respect the jumps and were not alarmed by the clatter as they hit the hurdles.

On September 5, 1949, Fred had his thirteenth ride in public over jumps, and his first catcall from the crowd.

Not all the people who go to National Hunt meetings are unbiased sportsmen with the interests of racing as a whole outweighing the feelings prompted by their pocket, but, as Fred will admit, he gave good reason for the venting of opinions that day.

His mount was once more old Carton, who generally was one of the safest jumpers in training. But Fred had driven to Folkestone in a state of apprehension. During the time he had been on the mend he had gone as a bystander to several meetings and watched jockeys fall, get up, shake themselves and walk away unharmed.

His own experience was two falls and two injuries, one of

them severe. He had decided that what he needed himself was three or four 'soft' falls. He didn't particularly want a fall that day at Folkestone, but he hoped that when it did come, it would be fairly easy and it would help him to regain his confidence.

They made Carton favourite and Fred settled him down last of the six runners, took the longest way round to avoid any trouble, passed one horse, which was in the process of being pulled up anyway, and finished last of the five runners left in the race. As he rode back to jump down from Carton in the paddock area, a large man came up and said in a loud voice that he had never seen such a windy ride in his life.

For all those who many times later saw Fred Winter drive a tiring horse into the last fence, conjuring a brave leap from an animal that had had enough and was quite capable of not rising at all, it seems hard now to visualise him as a rider who was frankly accused of being a coward.

A few weeks later he sat in the spartan, wooden weighing room at Hereford biting his nails and waiting to go out to ride War Cash, a recent purchase from Ireland owned by his godfather, Mr Tommy Morgan. There were 19 runners, quite enough for Hereford, and the ground was not inviting for anyone contemplating the prospect of a fall.

The bowler-hatted official shouted 'Jockeys please' and the first man to stand up and walk out of the wooden weighing room to the paddock was Jack Moloney who had finished second in the Grand National three times, on Easter Hero in 1929 (nearly twenty years before); on Gregalach in 1931; and on Delaneige in 1934, and now at the age of 52 was riding moderate horses round country meetings.

'Honest to God,' thought Fred, 'if that man can get up and walk out like that with no nerves at all, what the hell is wrong with you, Winter.'

Jack Moloney did in fact win that race on a four-year-old called Bachelor's Tonic. Fred finished well behind on War

26

Cash, who had probably not acclimatised yet after his transition from Ireland.

But four days later at Plumpton, he had his first ride in public for George Archibald on Dick the Gee, reputed to be a wonderful ride over hurdles. Fred did nothing wrong and neither did the horse.

They came into the last jump in Plumpton's short straight in front alongside that brave amateur-turned-professional, Dickie Black, riding the 11 to 8 favourite Pretence. Pretence was 'on the bit' and looking certain to win, but he made a mess of this jump and fell, leaving Fred and Dick the Gee to win comfortably.

The race had been handed to them on a plate, but it had two results. It was a great boost to Fred's morale, which was at its nadir, and it was seen by a man who was to play a vital part in Fred's career – Captain Ryan Price.

Fred had had his first ride for Ryan a few days earlier at Taunton on a horse called Smoke Piece and had been beaten a neck, thinking as he rode back to the unsaddling enclosure that this would probably be the last ride he would have for that particular stable. Ryan, who was not at the meeting, was, in fact, quite pleased with the way Smoke Piece ran. Fred's handling of Dick the Gee at Plumpton strengthened Ryan's opinion of his potential.

Fred had the 'easy' falls which he had been hoping for, and grew in confidence and ability. He had his first winner for Ryan Price at Newton Abbot on Boxing Day on Smoke Piece, and by the end of the year had ridden five winners.

The trainers who were now giving him rides included that shrewd, peppery character Gil Bennett. At Lingfield in December Fred rode the heavily-backed Papana for Bennett in a selling race. He had won on Papana at Sandown Park and was hopeful of his chances, but the race was to teach him a vital lesson about Lingfield which he never forgot.

At the top of the hill leading down to the turn into the straight, the leaders accelerated, and left Fred 'asleep' on

Papana. He turned into the straight ten lengths behind, and was beaten a length and a half into second place.

Gil Bennett could say a lot when roused but on this occasion he was remarkably cryptic. 'Well, boy,' he said, 'I don't know what you were up to, but they are saying a lot in the ring.' It was the last time Fred was caught napping there. Gil Bennett trusted him enough to put him up on Papana again in later races, as well as on other horses from the stable, and at Hurst Park in January Fred drove Papana to a two lengths victory.

At Birmingham on February 21 Fred had his thirteenth winner and his first in a race of any note. He won the Champion Trial Hurdle on Desir, a French-bred trained by Cliff Beechener. 'I do not think that National Spirit, Hatton's Grace, D.U.K.W. and Vatelys have anything to fear from the seven runners who contested today's race,' said Peter Willett in the *Sporting Chronicle*, and indeed it was Hatton's Grace who won the Champion Hurdle a fortnight later, with Desir unplaced.

But the writer also noted that at Birmingham Desir was 'splendidly ridden by young Fred Winter, who has reached the top ranks of N.H. jockeys in the space of one season'.

Fred was starting out at a time when there were some great jockeys in the game. A personal view is that the *general* standard of riding today is higher than it was. Young riders such as Josh Gifford, Johnny Haine, Jeff King, Barry Brogan and John Cook would hold their own in any generation.

The summers of 40 years ago were not necessarily composed of endless sunlit days as our elders would have us believe, but the fact remains that in the period during which Fred Winter was beginning to carve his way into racing history, there were some great riders in the game – Martin Molony, Bryan Marshall, the fearless Tim Molony, and over hurdles three excellent riders in Harry Sprague, Johnny Gilbert and Ken Mullins.

Fred had plenty to watch during racing, either from the stands or the back of a horse:

You can't ape anyone when you are developing a style. But you can learn a tremendous amount by watching the right people doing things. I loved watching Bryan Marshall. I thought he was out on his own as an all-rounder. You never saw him wrong at a fence or at a hurdle – a very good, stylish finisher and very strong; a wonderful man to watch on any course. He always knew the best way round, and the shortest way. I think if one could fault him at all, it was his mania for the inside, which he just couldn't leave. I did in fact see him lose quite a few races through waiting on the inside too long, but on the whole he was wonderful to watch. Another person well worth watching was Tim Molony – a most beautiful horseman. Horses never appeared to pull with him. He always said, well you know if you pull against them, they pull against you. Give them a long rein and don't fight against them and they won't fight against you, which most of the time is perfectly true. I was far too inclined to have a very short hold of the rein and fight against them.

Tim was riding for George Archibald at the time and I was able to ask him numerous questions, such as how did he get his horses to settle. He taught me a lot. He was terribly brave, and always kicking, kicking, going into a fence to try and get his horse to stand back and really jump. I think he was one of the bravest people I ever saw, certainly one of the toughest. His brother Martin was marvellous too, a real jockey, brilliant in every department.

Fred finished the 1949–50 season with 18 wins from 131 rides. He rode his first steeplechasing double at Cheltenham's April meeting, winning the Gratwicke Blagrave Memorial Challenge Cup on Priorit and the Holman Cup on Slender, both trained by Ryan Price. The first won by a length, and the second by a short head, and Fred's judgment of pace and his finishing power were noted.

The season which had started with him returning to racing a reluctant hero with an empty feeling inside him each time he rode out on to the course had blossomed and ended on a note of expectancy.

One man in particular had noted his progress, and was to prove a bigger factor in his racing life than anyone else. Ryan Price in those days had a small string of horses and was, like Fred, battling his way into the limelight. His wife Dorothy helped in the stable yard and often led a horse round the parade ring at the racecourse before going to watch the race beside Ryan and the owners in the grandstand.

For years, Ryan Price has had an instinctive eye for the young horse or one in which to him, but perhaps to few others, potential improvement was obvious.

This intense, hard-working man, is never happy to let one of his runners go on to the course unless he leads him down from the parade ring on to the track himself, as if to say 'Well there you, there's no more *I* can do. It's up to you now.'

His instinct certainly did not lead him astray when he picked out Fred Winter from among the struggling young riders in National Hunt racing in 1949. It was a partnership which lasted 16 years, and one of the most successful in the history of jumping.

CHAPTER FOUR

WIN IF YOU CAN

Fred returned for the annual reunion of the jumping fraternity at Newton Abbot at the start of August, 1950. In spite of the hard ground which made falling particularly uncomfortable, the jumping jockeys have always looked forward to the resumption on the West-country circuit.

There has always been swimming and sunbathing in the morning before the moments of truth on the racecourses at Devon and Exeter, high on the hills above the Exe Estuary, at Newton Abbot, and, until 1960, at that glorified point-to-point meeting at Buckfastleigh. For those without too much of a weight problem, high-spirited parties in the Globe Hotel at Newton Abbot, or the Queens at Torquay provided relaxation after racing.

Race meetings in the early part of the season were conveniently spaced out, and many jockeys spent two or three weeks in the West country before the tempo of the season began to quicken and the real slog from home to gallops to racecourse to home the week round began.

Probably the toughest part of a jockey's life besides the actual physical danger on the racecourse is the driving. Two or three hours driving to a meeting and two or three hours back becomes part of the day's work.

Over a period of ten months, Fred Winter usually covered some 50,000 miles, sometimes sharing the driving with a neighbouring trainer or jockey, many times alone. Jockeys, both flat and jumping, drive with the same élan which distinguishes them on horseback, and even going to the letter box on a Sunday evening, they find a reason to exceed speed limits obviously intended for less accomplished mortals.

Even so, 50,000 miles represents a tremendous number of hours behind a wheel – say about 1,200 hours, or 50 whole days out of the year. There is tension, too, about the business of setting out for a race meeting in the morning.

Most riders have a definite idea about how long it takes them to get from their home to each racecourse. They want to be there an hour before racing starts in case there is a chance of picking up any spare rides. They know just when they ought to leave the house.

For many this means a rapid breakfast (if they are eating), tearing round the house, snatching up form book, *Sporting Life*, overcoat, binoculars, a jangling of nerves as the phone rings at the last minute, a hurried kiss for the wife and children, and then eight or ten miles of flurried driving before they simmer down from this nervous peak at the start of the day.

Often a tense drive through fog during the winter months can end in the meeting not taking place, or the jockey arriving after three or more hours over the steering wheel, wishing he could take a couple of large Scotches in the bar to help him unwind rather than go out to ride some raw animal in a novices' 'chase.

Much of the driving back from winter meetings too, must be done under the worst possible conditions – in dusk, rain, fog or snow, and sometimes after a jockey is physically exhausted after covering more than 15 miles over fences and hurdles, or suffering a body-jerking fall.

To all this physical and mental strain must be added for many the torture of not being able to eat what they would like because of their continual battle against weight. A cup of tea and a boiled egg in the morning, tea and a piece of cake from the old boy who offers a limited and repetitive range of delicacies in the weighing room, and a carefully chosen evening meal, without too much liquid, is the routine for many riders.

Right: Fred Winter, C.B.E.
Below: Fred, aged 4½, rides out
with his father's string at Epsom

Halloween, the Contessa di Sant' Elia's perky little ex-hunter
on whom Fred won nine races, including two King George VI
Chases at Kempton Park

Fred was lucky for he never had to diet to keep his weight at around the 10 st 2 lb or 10 st 3 lb mark once he had ridden himself into fitness at the start of the season. Even so his eating programme was distinctly meagre in the eyes of anyone who enjoys his food.

He ate or drank just what he wanted, but this consisted of a cup of tea or two for breakfast, no lunch, a cup of tea and a piece of cake after racing, and a good meal with a few drinks in the evening.

Seven or eight times a season he might have to visit the Turkish baths in London in order to ride at less than 10 st 2 lb, and there he would see less fortunate colleagues for whom long periods in the baths were routine.

The 1950–51 season was the first one in which Fred really began to accumulate experience of both race-riding and of the stresses and strains of the life surrounding the actual moments in the saddle. He had a total of 221 rides, on a wide variety of courses, and 38 of them were winners. His only serious injury in 18 falls was a broken finger, collected when a horse called Noblest Roman, trained by Jack Anthony, fell with him at Kempton Park in March.

This season Lord Rosebery, whose colours are far better known on the flat than they are in National Hunt racing, decided to have a few jumpers in training with Harry Jelliss at Newmarket, and Fred was invited to ride for him.

This was a good prestige job to have, and Ryan Price and George Archibald, for whom Fred was now riding regularly, both agreed that he should take the retainer with Lord Rosebery in front of their own, while continuing to ride for them.

It was a successful association, as out of a limited number of rides in the famous primrose and rose hoops, Fred had five winners, including a double at Haydock Park in December on Garter Knight and Forethought.

The season was also notable for Fred's initiation into riding at Liverpool, in the Grand National. His mount was the eight-year-old Glen Fire, trained in Warwickshire by Syd Mercer.

The tension in the jockeys' room before going out to ride in the National is always severe, even in these days when the fences are somewhat easier than they were then.

For Fred it was not made any better by the leg-pulling of fellow jockeys such as Tim Molony and Glen Kelly, who had themselves ridden Glen Fire in the past and were now prepared to bet Fred that he would not get as far as Becher's Brook first time round – the sixth fence.

In the event, Fred and Glen Fire survived an enormous pile up at the first fence when 11 horses either fell or were brought down (a photograph shows Glen Fire ten yards after the jump leaping again to clear a fallen horse and rider) and they reached the Canal Turn, two beyond Bechers, before, in Fred's words, they 'came unstuck completely'. Neither horse nor rider was injured and Fred duly collected from his weighing room colleagues.

By the end of this season, in which Fred finished well up the list of winning jockeys, with only Tim Molony, Bryan Marshall, Arthur Thompson and Martin Molony above him, he was developing some of the characteristics which were to hallmark his riding for many seasons – his judgment of pace, his skill in selecting the shortest route from the start to the winning post on any shape of track, his unflinching courage in driving a horse into the last fence, his powerful finish :

Whenever I first went to a course, I would go round it on foot slowly, and I mean slowly. You must really study a course before you ride on it. At the turns or anywhere you might be able to make a bit of ground, I would study it seriously from several angles, and see the best way round.
I think the inside has tremendous value, not only as the shortest way. You have far less interference from other horses with only the rail on one side of you, and you get a much

*clearer view of the jumps. I loathed going into an obstacle
with a horse on either side of me, because there is a good
chance one or the other would make a mistake and quite
possibly jump into you. When you follow the inside, you
find that nearly every horse has a tendency to jump away
from the wing, and therefore the horse you are following will
always leave you a clear view and the horse beside you won't
jump into you.*

*If anything is going to happen, you may jump into him,
which is far less bother and in fact if you do it badly he will
be rather inclined to help you keep on your feet. You have
got far more chance of keeping a horse properly balanced on
a turn if you have the rail, and I think there are very few
courses where it is not worth a couple of lengths.*

*The only time the inside is not in your favour is when the
ground is heavy and then it pays to go fairly wide and find
a piece of ground that has not been chewed up. There were
times when I went disproportionately wide to find better
ground, even on little courses like Newton Abbot, but then
you find your horse striding away on decent going while
those on the inside are stuck down in the mud.*

*On the whole though, the inside is best. I always like to get
on it and stay there until the time comes to pull out, if
necessary, to get a clear run to make your challenge.*

Back from a month's holiday in the South of France at
the start of the 1951–52 season, Dave Dick and Fred headed
for Newton Abbot in Fred's Jaguar, the first good car he
acquired once he started to ride plenty of winners. They had
spent the last few weeks water-skiing during the daytime and
getting acquainted with the local feminine talent in the even-
ings – a holiday pattern which lasted until Fred gave up
bachelorhood.

By a few minutes after three o'clock on the first afternoon
of the new season it looked as though they had between them
landed the first two winners.

Dave had led from start to finish on Miss Dorothy Paget's Kellsboro' Lad in the novices' 'chase which opened the programme. In the second race Fred was just challenging at the last hurdle on the 2 to 1 favourite Ocean Gem, trained by George Archibald, when he fell and Fred broke a collar bone, which put him out of business for a month.

When he resumed riding early in September, Fred was not long in bringing home his first winner – a popular horse called Campari who was just setting out on a long career which was to involve him in 62 races and 13 wins.

This win was at Fontwell Park and a few days later at Plumpton Fred had his first treble: on Vingt Sept and Campari both trained by Ryan Price, and Arrius, trained in Kent by Ernie Long.

Two of these winners on the sharp little Plumpton course were in steeplechases and the only remarkable thing about this is that it was not long afterwards that Fred gave up riding fences at Plumpton.

'Sorry, sir, finished riding over fences there years ago. Ask John Lehane or Michael or Tim,' he would say when a trainer asked him to take a ride in a 'chase at Plumpton. Fred's reason for this was that in one series of about a dozen rides, he failed to finish the course 11 times. Ryan Price eventually agreed that he should stop riding over fences there.

Self preservation or commonsense? Outwardly Fred showed no signs of being 'windy' now when riding on other courses but it is probable that if he had not taken this step, his mental attitude as he went out to ride in a steeplechase at Plumpton might one day have ended in an almost self-induced fall which could have cut short his story.

Throughout the season Fred produced a steady flow of winners and at Kempton Park in January, 1952, he passed the 50 mark for the first time with another victory on Campari. The thought was gradually dawning on people that here was a champion jockey of the future, and one of the first to voice it was Richard Baerlein, then writing for the *Evening Standard* and now racing correspondent of *The Observer* and *The Guardian*.

Baerlein said:

'Practically unknown to the public two years ago, but probable champion National Hunt jockey within two years, Winter is the man to break Molony's run... He rides beautifully throughout a race and it is a pleasure to watch him gradually bringing his mount into a challenging position. He often wins his races between the last two fences and then rides a finish worthy of a flat race jockey.'

At the big Cheltenham meeting in March, Fred was involved in an incident incredibly similar to that better remembered hair-raising moment some 10 years later when Mandarin lost his bridle in the Grand Steeplechase de Paris. This time, he was riding the gallant little grey horse Shaef, trained by Jack Gosden.

It was a good Gold Cup. It brought out Miss Paget's brilliant young horse Mont Tremblant, the fast but erratic Galloway Braes, Nagara, winner of a Grand Steeplechase, Lord Bicester's great horse Silver Fame, now reaching the end of a great career, Freebooter, who had won a Grand National, and E.S.B. who was to win one, Knock Hard, who won the Gold Cup the following year, the popular Greenogue – for all-round quality it was one of the best Gold Cup fields for years.

Shaef started fourth favourite in this field of stars, and all went well until jumping the water the first time, a horse cannoned in him. In the scramble as they landed the far side, Shaef's bridle was knocked completely off his head and left hanging round his mouth.

Fortunately for Fred, a fairly tight nose band helped to keep the bit in Shaef's mouth, but he was faced with the prospect of riding nearly three miles over fences in one of the most competitive races of the season without letting go of Shaef's head in case the bit fell out of his mouth. In spite of this restraint, Shaef ran a fine race to finish second, 10 lengths behind Mont Tremblant, and with some high class opponents behind him.

Two days later at Hurst Park Fred was seen in public for the first time on a horse with whom his name was to be linked for the next five years – Halloween. This was a horse who did not generate perhaps the following of an Arkle, but had a tremendous band of admirers who would travel long distances to see him.

Halloween won a total of 17 races and nearly £10,000 but at the time that Fred first rode him he was a problem horse. No professional jockey had succeeded in completing a race on him. Bought as a highly successful point-to-point horse by the wealthy Contessa di Sant' Elia from his owner rider Captain Dick Smalley for £8,000, Halloween had fallen with that competent horseman Dick Francis in the Grand Sefton Trial Chase at Hurst Park in October, and then gave Desmond Dartnall a first fence fall at Newbury in November.

His ex-owner was invited to ride him in his next two races, and won both of them. Dick Smalley was not stylish but on Halloween he was certainly effective. The two races he now won were both amateurs' events at Newbury, but Bill Wightman, who trained him, had much more ambitious plans for this potential champion, and it was felt that a professional just had to be found who could complete a race with Halloween. Fred was invited to ride him in the Grand National Trial Chase at Hurst Park.

I went to Dick Smalley and said what's the secret of success, what do you do? He said I do nothing. Just sit completely still. So I went out on Halloween in this four miles one furlong race at Hurst Park and I sat like a complete mouse the whole way. He won running away.

It was the start of a tremendously successful partnership during which Fred won the King George VI Chase on Halloween in both 1952 and 1954.

By March 10, Fred was within striking distance of Tim Molony in the jockeys' championship table – only 11 wins behind. But on March 22 a horse called Botany Bay dived through the wing of the sixth fence with him in a novices' 'chase at Newbury, and Fred suffered a cracked arm.

He tried hard to induce the doctors to pass him fit to ride in the Grand National a fortnight later as he was booked to ride Irish Lizard, Lord Sefton's horse who was usually a magnificent ride round the Aintree course. As it happened, Irish Lizard was brought down this time at the first fence, but Fred was not in the saddle and it was not until April 12 that he rode another winner, at Newton Abbot.

Fifteen more winners came within the last weeks of the season, but the two injuries, first a broken collar bone and then a cracked arm, had ruined Fred's hope of becoming champion jockey in only his third full season. Tim Molony finished the year a tantalising one victory short of the century, and Fred's total was 85.

But all the evidence was there. Given reasonable luck in this hazardous game, here was a champion jockey of the not too distant future.

His singleness of purpose – to ride as many winners as possible – was the biggest factor in his favour in his effort to head the jockeys' list. But very early in his career, Fred found that not all the people he encountered in racing were entirely honest.

It was inevitable that someone in Fred's position should have to brush shoulders with the crooked and the dishonest in a sport which involves huge sums of money. Whenever the prizes are as great as those which the betting market in this country can offer, people will try to bend the rules to their own advantage or stoop to downright dishonesty in order to increase the odds in their own favour.

There is in fact, far less dishonesty in racing than the man in the street likes to believe. It gives the punter something of a thrill to think that he has detected a case of 'cheating', and often the events which he thought he observed can be attributed to something quite innocent, such as the failure of a piece of equipment, a hefty bump collected by a horse just as he starts his challenge, or that factor that it is almost impossible to assess before a race – the horse is not feeling at his best.

The Americans have spent a great deal of money in publicising the fact that their racing is well policed and as honest as it can be made, and certainly crookedness there is far more difficult than it is in many countries. But still the American backer likes to think that he personally is capable of seeing what 'They' are up to.

This is true of backers all round the world, and against this background it is infrequent for a man to be identified by the public and by racing professionals as one who is completely trustworthy. It happened with Gordon Richards, and quite early in his career it happened with Fred Winter.

Many people who have had dealings with him have been aware of his inherent honesty. It is not often that this feeling is conveyed to a majority of those who may bet on a jockey's mounts.

Peter O'Sullevan summed up the case for Fred in an article in the *Racing Review* in 1953 when he said, 'Ask one of the "boys" who are inclined to view a race, darkly, through the recesses of their pockets, what they think of Winter and you'll hear "with Freddie you are sure to get a run". When even these demolishers of reputations admit to the possibility of integrity, a blow has been struck on behalf of the riding fraternity.'

Not long after he had started riding over jumps Fred agreed, at the request of the owner, not to win on a horse running at a west country meeting, but the experience made

40

him so unhappy that he resolved never to be involved in anything like this again.

He thought the best way to do the job was to be left many lengths, which he achieved, and after making up the ground steadily, and feeling that the whole world was watching him, he finished fifth. Next time out the horse won at a Midlands meeting with another jockey in the saddle and there was immediately a stewards' enquiry.

Fred was at the meeting and was called before the stewards. Fred Withington, one of the outstanding racing officials of the era, told him before he went in to face them : 'You have nothing to worry about. Just tell the truth.' Fred said that the horse had been left many lengths in its previous race, and the stewards accepted his explanation, but he resolved there and then not to have anything more to do with this type of machination.

There was an occasion later when he was asked in the paddock not to win on a well known selling chaser, whom he had ridden to victory in his previous race at a London meeting. Fred turned to the trainer and said that under no circumstances would he stop the horse and he could tell the owner to go and do what he liked with himself. To his great satisfaction, the horse won very comfortably.

There was a similar incident a season or two later when an owner for whom Fred had ridden a number of winners, indicated that he should give his horse an easy race in a novices' hurdle. Fred won three-quarters of a length, and the infuriated owner said that he would never ride again for him.

This came at a time when Fred was recovering from a serious injury and trying to re-establish his confidence, so that it was a particularly unwelcome blow.

Two months later the owner suddenly asked him if he would ride two horses for him at a major meeting, one of them being the horse on which he had the temerity to win earlier.

Fred accepted ('I don't believe one man's money is any

41

worse than another's, and anyway there is no point in cutting off your nose to spite your face') and the sequel was that in a tremendous battle Fred was beaten a neck, justifiably objected and was awarded the race.

I was asked to give horses easy races after that but they did not have much chance when they started. If at any time through a race I found that the horse was within striking distance and had a chance of winning, then I would go and do my best to win.

Years later when Fred started training, the same tenets applied and the instructions have always been: 'Win if you can.'

CHAPTER FIVE

ALL HORSES CAN JUMP—
IN DIFFERENT WAYS

At the start of each season for perhaps a month Ryan Price would ask Fred to go down to Findon to do some schooling over jumps. Fred always swears that this was only because Ryan wanted to make sure that his nerve had not gone.

Perhaps this was true, because after that the trainer was seldom insistent on Fred making the long journey down to Sussex in order to do some schooling.

Perhaps it was because he was no good at schooling, was Fred's interpretation of this:

It was obviously very essential, but I just didn't enjoy it, and thought it rather a waste of time. It's just a matter of getting a horse from one side of an obstacle to the other and with him knowing how he got there. I was far happier for someone else to produce the finished article for me to ride on the course, even if I had never seen the horse before. Certainly there was seldom anything to complain about the way Ryan's horses jumped on the course.

Syd Warren used to produce some brilliant jumpers over hurdles, though the jumps he schooled them over were so small that you wouldn't think it would make any difference. Neville Crump schooled his horses in a loose school, and they were all brilliant, but I think the best schooled horses when I was riding were Fulke Walwyn's. Look at the people who used to school them – Bryan Marshall and Dave Dick mostly. Bryan was a wonderful horseman; and with Dave I believe they really used to enjoy it. Fulke is a perfectionist. If it isn't right he sends them back again. All horses can jump, of course – in different ways.

During the 1952–53 season, 41 horses failed to jump as well as Fred hoped, and 41 times he hit the ground at speeds of around 30 miles per hour. Yet it proved the most successful season that any National Hunt jockey had ever had. He was champion jockey with 121 winners, and this record stood until Josh Gifford, also riding principally for Ryan Price, rode 122 winners during the 1966–67 season.

From the start of the season until the end, Fred was competely fit, in spite of 41 falls. The weather was remarkably kind and there was no serious interruption of racing, and Ryan Price had his horses in such superb form throughout the season that he also established a new record for a trainer of 76 victories in a year.

On a number of occasions Fred was caught up in a flurry of falling horses, hit the ground hard, and was the only jockey to walk away unhurt.

Everything just clicked into place the whole way through the season. There was an occasion when luck remained on his side even though he had made what could have been a costly mistake.

Riding E.S.B. at Towcester, Fred forgot to keep a check on the number of times it was necessary to go round to complete the three miles steeplechase course :

It was the first time I had ever ridden in a three miles 'chase there, though that was no excuse. We had planned to wait with E.S.B., and when we came to the bottom of the hill up to the winning post the second time, I had him in about fifth place, thinking we had to go round again. Then I suddenly realised all the other jockeys were working away like mad, and I had to do something in a hurry.
To cap it all, E.S.B. hit the last fence hard, but we scrambled home a couple of lengths in front.

A contributory factor to Fred's own success this season was a horrible accident which happened to his best friend, Dave Dick. Riding Miss Dorothy Paget's Prince of Denmark at Cheltenham in November, Dave hit the rails and severely damaged his left ankle.

The accident resulted in a court case against the racecourse, in which Dave was awarded £5,000, but he did not ride again that season, and Miss Paget, whose horses were then trained by Fulke Walwyn, was without a jockey.

In addition to Mont Tremblant, who had won the previous season's Gold Cup, beating Fred on Shaef, Miss Paget had a highly promising year younger half brother to him, Lanveoc Poulmic. This horse was brilliant, but he had an unpleasant habit of cocking up his behind as he came over a fence and giving his rider an unexpected blow which made it difficult to stay in the saddle.

The previous season, Bryan Marshall, having ridden a good many winners for Miss Paget, lost his job with her after being beaten half a length on Lanveoc Poulmic in a novices' hurdle at Sandown Park.

Midway through the 1952–53 season, Miss Dorothy Paget sent word that she would like Fred Winter to ride her horses, and at Sandown Park in December he had his first ride on Lanveoc Poulmic in a 2½m. novices' 'chase. Starting at 5/2 on, the five-year-old went into the lead three fences from home and won by eight lengths from Bryan Marshall on Approval.

Fred got on well with Lanveoc Poulmic, and won five races on him that season. His only defeat was the result of one of Fred's most frightening experiences. He was lucky to come out of it alive.

At Kempton Park on Boxing Day, Lanveoc Poulmic, a 6 to 1 on favourite for the last race in front of a huge holiday crowd, hit the last fence hard and Fred had no chance of staying in the saddle. But one of his feet was still tangled in the iron, and the stirrup leather was twisted round his ankle.

45

Hitting the fence had brought him almost to a standstill, but then he started getting back into his stride again, and I thought – this is it, this is the worst thing that can happen. I remember staying terribly cool and reaching up to grab hold of the bridle as near to the bit as I could get. I heaved with all my strength and weight, and pulled his head round so that all he could do was go in two or three tight circles and then come to a standstill. I was still hanging upside down and I couldn't get my leg out of the iron even then until a spectator ran out and picked me up.

Dorothy Paget was an extraordinary woman, with looks to frighten a polar bear. Fred rode many winners for her that season, but at the end he knew no more about her than at the start. Always surrounded by two or three secretaries (one of them later married Charlie Smirke) she said little to her jockeys in the paddock, though she was always generous to them after they had won a race.

On a day when Fred had six rides for Miss Paget at Sandown Park, which resulted in three winners, two seconds and a third, she demonstrated her unpredictability. Fred finished second in the opening event on Festival III and when he walked into the paddock for his second mount, which was Lanveoc Poulmic, he stood roughly in the same place as he had for the first race.

But when Miss Paget arrived with her entourage, she swept past him like a ship in full sail, completely ignored him, and went to the furthest end of the paddock. Fred sheepishly followed her and later asked one of the secretaries what it was all about. 'Oh, don't worry,' she replied. 'That was an unlucky place to stand because we were beaten in the first race.'

On the day when Fred had had such an alarming fall at Kempton Park with Lanveoc Poulmic, little Halloween gave him his most important win so far, in the King George VI Chase. With Fred sitting still and letting the ex-hunter work it out for himself, he had already won the Grand Sefton Trial Chase at Hurst Park in October from Galloway Braes, Greenogue and E.S.B., and survived a couple of mistakes to win a three miles 'chase at Kempton Park in November.

For the King George VI Chase, Halloween was a 7/4 favourite to beat a high class field, and coming to challenge Mont Tremblant at the last fence, he took the lead on the flat and sped away to a length win.

It had not been without its frightening moments for Fred. At the open ditch on the opposite side of the course to the Kempton stands, Halloween took off far too soon and looked certain to Fred to land on top of the fence. But he gave an extraordinary buck in mid-air. For a moment there seemed to be no horses in front of Fred, but that extra 'jump' in the air got them safely over.

Halloween could never win a Cheltenham Gold Cup. This gay little horse did win races at Cheltenham, but in the Gold Cup, the pace that is turned on from the top of the hill just over half a mile from home seemed to be too good for him, though he was always running on at the finish.

This particular season he finished second in the Gold Cup to Galloway Braes after being fifth two fences from home and sprinting up the hill to be beaten five lengths. The following year he was beaten eight lengths into third place by Four Ten, in 1955 he was second to Gay Donald, beaten 10 lengths, and finally at the age of 11 he was third to Limber Hill.

Fred's first winner in his fabulous 1952–53 season had been Sea Bird, trained by Ryan Price, at Newton Abbot on August 15, and 14 of his first 16 winners were for Ryan.

By mid-season they were calling him 'Winner-a-day Winter,' and by the end of February Fred looked certain, or as certain as anything can be in steeplechasing, to be the first rider to score a century since Fred Rees in 1924.

His only winner at the Cheltenham National Hunt Festival meeting at the start of March was Sy Oui in the

Mildmay of Flete Challenge Cup, but at Hurst Park three days later he won the Triumph Hurdle on a tough individual called Clair Soleil, who had been bought by Ryan Price for Mr Gerry Judd only the day before the race for £5,000 from Mme François Dupré.

Unknown to Fred, Clair Soleil when taken out on the racecourse the day before the Triumph for a school had refused to jump, which was no recommendation at all for a horse about to take part in the most hotly contested race of the year for four-year-old hurdlers.

Fred soon began to have some idea of the character he was astride, however, when they were standing at the gate as the starter called the roll. Clair Soleil, black as a funeral horse and with a roguish sort of eye, leaned over and grabbed champion jockey Tim Molony by the leg as he sat quietly on the favourite Otari.

Clair Soleil got a kick in the ribs and a clout from Fred's whip for this effort. When he set off in the race all went well until there was some jostling on the rather tight turn passing the stands. Clair Soleil, resenting being squeezed for room, suddenly turned his head and grabbed the horse alongside him by the neck.

At this, Fred lost his temper and really took hold of Clair Soleil, driving him into every hurdle with the result that the horse started to concentrate and jump brilliantly. Coming to the last hurdle Otari looked a certainty but Fred, driving Clair Soleil for all he was worth, forced the French horse up to win by half length.

This brought Fred's total of winners for the season to 98, and the whole racing world was waiting for him to ride his next two winners. Number 99 came the same day on Nordest in a selling hurdle, but the following week Fred could ride nothing but seconds and thirds, and he was unplaced at Sandown Park on the Saturday on Nuage Dore, favourite for the Imperial Cup.

Half an hour later Fred rode an inspired race on Air

Wedding in the three miles handicap chase, leading over the last fence to be headed on the flat and then came again to win by a short head. The crowd roared their approval and rushed to the unsaddling enclosure to welcome him back.

Fred described it then as the greatest and proudest day of his career. The Queen and the Queen Mother watched his triumph from the quaint green and white wooden Royal box next to the Members Stand. He was asked to go to the Royal box after this historic victory, but as he was due to ride Father Thames in the next event (which he also won), the Queen and the Queen Mother came down to the paddock to congratulate him.

The Queen told him she thought it was a great achievement to ride a hundred winners so early in the season and wished him luck in trying to beat Fred Rees' record. Fred explained that he had been very lucky in escaping injury through the season.

And it went on.

In the last few weeks of the season Fred was seldom out of the news, and he finished at Fontwell Park on May 25 champion jockey for the first time with 121 winners. His last winner, Gribun, was appropriately trained by Ryan Price, to whom he felt he owed a great deal. If ever a man was riding on a cloud it was that day at Sandown Park, when the public flocked to cheer him.

Certainly no steeplechase jockey has ever established himself in the hearts of the racing public as Fred had done.

But as every rider knows who puts at stake his life every time he walks from the weighing room to the paddock to ride in a jumping race, no one in this game is exempt from ill fortune. It can grind a man further and further into despondency with a never ending series of accidents. It can suddenly deflate a man when he is carrying all before him.

On the day that Fred won on Gribun at Fontwell, he was also successful on Cent Francs, trained by Syd Warren, in the selling hurdle. Ryan Price bought Cent Francs at the auction, and he was Fred's first ride at Newton Abbot on the opening day of the next season in a novices' 'chase. Cent Francs fell at the first fence and Fred broke his leg.

I had absolutely no pain whatever as I sat on the grass and began to get up. Then I could feel the bone grating and I knew I had broken my leg. It still wasn't hurting – just this grating sensation in my boot. I yelled to the ambulance men to be careful as I had broken my leg, which they didn't believe, but they did as they were told and picked me up carefully. I still don't know how it happened, because I don't remember Cent Francs kicking me or anything. So there I was, one moment starting off the season full of confidence, and the next moment being carted off to hospital with a broken leg.
I think this really is a wonderful aspect of this game. No matter how successful you are you can come to earth again very, very quickly. Any fellow who starts getting big-headed is only asking for trouble, because along comes something which slaps him down in very smart time.

CHAPTER SIX

SLAPPED DOWN

It is doubtful if Fred *had* been getting big-headed, but he was certainly slapped down decisively, and it was a full year before he rode again – a year of pain and continued frustration, a year during which he fell in love with and almost immediately lost the girl he was later to marry, a year in which he felt nearer to suicide than at any stage of his life before or since.

It was a compound fracture of the left leg, a really messy job which presented the doctors with many problems. Fred was taken to Torquay Hospital and his own doctor in London, Dr Aiden Redmond, was contacted.

The next day the doctor arrived at Torquay with a special Daimler ambulance ('more like a hearse than an ambulance, I thought' said Fred afterwards), and Fred was driven 250 miles back to the London Clinic where he was X-rayed by Mr Bill Tucker, the orthopaedic surgeon who has skilfully handled the injuries of many sportsmen.

Because part of the leg bone was sticking through the skin and had caused an unpleasant wound, it was impossible for the leg to be re-set for nearly three weeks while the flesh around the injury healed. During this period, Fred was in no pain at all, had plenty of visitors and attention to cheer him up, and fondly imagined that the leg was healing nicely under the plaster that had been put on at Newton Abbot.

The moment of truth came when it was decided that the leg was now ready for a proper re-setting of the bone, and the plaster cast had to come off.

Unhappily for Fred, when the plaster had been put on wet, it had been applied direct to his leg without anyone remembering to shave off the hairs.

The pain which resulted when the plaster was removed, and with it almost every hair on Fred's leg, was far worse than anything he experienced before or after.

Three bone grafts were necessary and a month after the fall Fred was allowed to leave hospital on a stretcher and to go to his parents' home at Southfleet. The leg stayed in plaster for three months, and when it did see the light of day again it was not a pretty sight, thin and wasted, with nasty hanging flesh.

Fred was fitted with a caliper and got around with the aid of two sticks. He did daily exercises to strengthen the leg, and then early in December the caliper was taken off and he tried to ride out with his father's string one morning. It was a disappointing moment.

The wound, which from time to time still discharged matter, was on the inside of the leg and made it painful to sit on the horse. When the animal jigged to one side and Fred gripped as usual with his knees, his weakened leg shook like jelly.

There were optimistic reports in the press that Fred would ride again by Christmas time, then in the New Year, but in spite of heat treatment and swimming three times a week the leg was not making good progress.

It was still discharging matter and pieces of bone (the last pieces of bone came away from the leg almost nine years after the accident), and by early in March Fred finally decided that there was no point in hoping that he would be able to ride again that season.

He watched the racing at the big Cheltenham meeting on television, and then went up to Aintree with Dave Dick for three days for a change of scene and to see the Grand National.

They stayed at the Adelphi Hotel, a place which has seen

much racing history and which was now to play an important part in Fred's own story.

The massive hotel in Lime Street has been the traditional scene of some mammoth, mad, post-Grand National parties staged by the owners of winners of the great race and attended by hundreds of people – some remotely connected with the winning stable and some not even that.

The bills have been enormous but so, on occasions, has the damage, as high spirited jockeys and others relaxed after the tension of the National. On one occasion a piano was propelled through a window and hit the pavement below with an awe-inspiring chord which must have been heard in Birkenhead.

The breakfast room at the Adelphi was a reasonably quiet place on Grand National morning as Fred and Dave sat looking at the papers and discussing the big race, in which Dave was to ride Miss Paget's eleven-year-old Legal Joy.

Into the room walked an elderly woman accompanied by a tall, slim girl, wearing a white high-necked sweater which showed off her best lines. Fred stopped in his conversation as if he had been shot.

It appears to have been a classic case of love at first sight.

At this stage Fred did not know who the girl was, but that evening after Royal Tan had won the National, Fred found out that she was called Diana Pearson, that her parents lived at Brailsford in Derbyshire, and that she was just about to set out on a round-the-world tour.

Fred, joining in the party spirit, consumed a fair amount of drink that evening, and recalls bumping into Diana in a hotel corridor and informing her (in spite of the fact that his only connection with her to date was that they had shared the same breakfast room with several dozen other people) that he intended accompanying her on her travels.

The following day a more subdued Fred asked a friend to introduce him properly to Diana, and by now completely starstruck, he managed to extract her phone number from her. Travelling back to London by train, he exasperated Dave Dick by continually talking about Diana, and as soon as he got home he phoned the number she had given him.

Either Diana was playing it cautiously or Fred had written the number down incorrectly, but it proved that there was no such number. More sleuthing was needed before he tracked her down again.

Fred said he absolutely had to see her again. Diana said she was going up to London to shop in preparation for her world trip, and it was quite impossible. By persistent arguing Fred got a begrudging date for lunch on Monday, and he headed for London, where for the next four days he followed Diana round as she shopped, carrying parcels.

This idyllic existence came to an end when Diana returned to Derbyshire on Thursday, but she invited him to her farewell party which was to take place at the Dorchester Hotel on the Saturday, before she departed on the boat train from Victoria the next day.

Fred booked himself into the Dorchester and went to the party with a sinking heart as he knew that in a few hours Diana would be disappearing out of his life again for many months. He was one of the small crowd who saw her off at Victoria the next morning.

I didn't go as far as tears, but I felt very bad indeed. As soon as she went off I went to the morning service at Westminster Cathedral and then went home on the train. I have never felt so bad in my life. I really did feel like throwing myself off the train. I was so depressed, with the conglomeration of the leg being so painful and taking so long to mend, and this girl I had fallen in love with going away.

A period of depression and boredom followed. The start of the next jumping season was nine weeks away and it was obvious that the leg still needed plenty of time. Fred started taking flying lessons at Rochester air field, but it all seemed pointless and quite frightening too, learning to fly in a plane which danced around at the slightest puff of wind, and in which the throttle worked the opposite way to a set of reins.

He gave it up after five lessons, and went to stay in Morocco with his sister Sheila, whose husband worked there for an American firm.

After five weeks of lying in the sun and being well looked after, he flew from Casablanca to the South of France to join Dave Dick on familiar holidaying ground. Fred tried his hand again at the sport he and Dave enjoyed so much, water skiing, but each time the flesh round his leg wound became inflamed and began to discharge again. After a short while, he went home and set about trying to get fit again.

He went to Newton Abbot on July 31 at the start of the new season, not knowing whether his leg was really ready again for the exertions of race riding, though he had by now been riding out most mornings. It was still fairly painful to ride.

The public obviously expected him to re-start with a winner. His very first mount, Fatum, was made a 5 to 4 on favourite, but he was beaten half a length by Mr Edward Cazalet on Diego Rubio.

In spite of this, Fred returned to the jockeys' room feeling elated. It had gone much better than he had dared to hope. An hour later he had his second ride, in the selling hurdle on Triple A, trained by Ryan Price, and he was back in business. Triple A beat 27 other horses comfortably.

It was the start of a busy season in which only one other rider had more mounts than him, and in which that rider, Tim Molony, managed to defeat him for the jockeys' championship – but for the last time.

By now Fred had had over 1,200 rides over jumps, but few people realise the strain that can build up in a National Hunt jockey's mind when he thinks he is due for a fall and wants it to be an easy one when it comes.

When things are going right, jockeys begin to worry.

A rider who has had 60 or 70 rides without a fall, may go out thinking that the crash when it comes will be something out of the ordinary.

Race-riding over jumps is a dangerous business and hitting the ground, without time to prepare oneself in the way that a parachutist does, from the back of a falling horse which may roll on you for good measure, is a way of life which puts great pressure on the individual. Superstitions build up.

Fred himself found a great deal of help in his religion. A Catholic by birth, he attended morning service every Sunday and found that prayer gave him renewed strength in his particularly tough walk of life:

I would not describe myself as a deeply religious person, but I seldom miss going to church, and it has been an enormous help to me. I think it would be fair to say that one was living with fear the whole time, particularly just after I broke my leg. It helped to be able to get down and pray for courage – which I did quite often.

Fred had his first fall this season with Nuage Dore, normally a good jumper, in a conditions race at Devon and Exeter. Nuage Dore was an 11 to 8 on favourite, and he fell on the far side of the course, giving Fred a long walk back to the stands through the heather, but he was completely sound in wind and limb. The fall gave him renewed confidence.

At Hurst Park in October, Fred teamed up again with Halloween and finished second in the Grand Sefton Trial Chase, beaten ten lengths by Son of Marie, who was receiving over two stones. Three weeks later Halloween won a three miles 'chase at Cheltenham with Fred in the saddle, and he set up a sequence of four victories, which included his second King George VI Chase at Kempton Park, beating the unpredictable Galloway Braes, Mariner's Log, a horse who never quite lived up to his early promise, and the popular Crudwell.

Fred did not subscribe to the view that there is often one jockey for one horse. He believed that a rider should be able to adapt himself to the requirements of each horse once he had found the key to the animal – to sit still if that is the answer, or to push and shove the whole time, to give the horse 'the office' coming into a fence and try to get him to take off when you want him to.

But looking back on Halloween's record it certainly seemed that Fred was the only professional jockey who had found the key to Halloween.

During the 1951–52 and 1952–53 seasons, Fred had six rides on Halloween and won five times. During the next season when Fred was injured and out of action, Halloween was ridden by four different riders, ran eight times, and won one small race at Wincanton. Then Fred returned and he won four out of seven races on Halloween in the 1954–55 season.

There was undoubtedly something that worked between Fred and Halloween, even though they finished only second again in the 1953 Cheltenham Gold Cup, won by Gay Donald.

It was not a bad Cheltenham meeting for Fred, however, for he won the Champion Hurdle on Clair Soleil, who went through the season unbeaten in three races – and a fortnight before Cheltenham, Diana returned from her round-the-world tour.

Like Fred, Clair Soleil had spent the previous season out of action, though for rather different reasons. Ryan Price had decided that Clair Soleil's bad temper and his general antipathy to any person or animal who crossed his path had to be cured, and so Mr Gerry Judd's black horse was 'cut', or in Racing Calendar terms, added to the list of geldings.

Some leg trouble had also contributed to Clair Soleil's

57

absence the previous season, but he came back a stronger and more powerful horse, who was soon to establish himself as a 14 lb better animal in really heavy going than when the going was 'on top'. The tougher the conditions the better he was and this season he carried top weight in the Victory Hurdle in appallingly heavy ground at Manchester and won by ten lengths.

In spite of his operation, Clair Soleil was still a character – even a desperate character. Sometimes he would go down on his knees and try to eat the ground. Fred once remarked that when Clair Soleil was 90 per cent fit he was a great horse, and when he was 100 per cent fit he was a little bit mad.

The Champion Hurdle this year was a tremendous race, with 21 runners, including Sir Ken, who was trying for his fourth consecutive win, and the heavily-backed Irish horse Stroller, who had won his two previous races in the highest possible class.

Prince Charlemagne, a good horse on the flat, led them at a great gallop from the start; flattening most of the hurdles, and then almost a mile from home, made a final blunder and dropped back, leaving Fred and Clair Soleil in front. Up to this point, Fred had not been having a happy ride. Clair Soleil was sulking somewhat, objecting to the rattling pace at which he was being fetched along, but finding himself in front he suddenly cheered up, pricked his ears and went on in the lead taking a great deal more interest in the proceedings.

Fred was now in a difficult position, because his instructions had been to wait and come with a late run. But in a race like the Champion Hurdle, run from end to end at a tremendous gallop, you cannot afford to give away ground once it has been gained, and he decided that all he could do was to make the best of his way home.

With Stroller and the good northern-trained horse Cruachan closing on him, Fred drove Clair Soleil into the last hurdle with all the power he could muster. Halfway up that searching hill to the Cheltenham winning post, Stroller got his head in front, but Fred somehow drew a last effort from the tough horse under him, and at the post Clair Soleil was inches in front.

Fred rode back to a withering blast from Ryan Price who wanted to know why the hell he had disobeyed orders and not waited with the horse for a late challenge. It was a point on which they never agreed afterwards, for Ryan insisted that Clair Soleil had a brilliant turn of finishing speed, and Fred considered him an out-and-out stayer without much acceleration.

I must say that the way in which the race was run had a lot to do with me being in front so far from home. I think I had three rockets from Ryan the whole time I was riding for him, and really it was the most marvellous association between a trainer and a jockey that they could wish for. Apart from the times when I had obviously done something wrong and he let one know in no uncertain terms, he never blamed you for being beaten. He enjoys winning a race at Devon and Exeter just as much as winning a big race at Cheltenham.

Fred had another important hurdles win for Ryan Price before the end of this season, on Nuage Dore in the Liverpool Hurdle on Grand National Day. It was his second win in a hurdle race at Liverpool, but still he had not won a steeple-chase there, and his Grand National mount, Oriental Way, trained by Vincent O'Brien, got no further than the eleventh fence before he fell.

With only a fortnight to go before the end of the season, Fred was right in the front line for the jockeys' championship. On May 16 a double on Vermillon and Clontarf at Wye brought him up level with Tim Molony, four times champion in the past six seasons. A few days later Fred was in the lead when Clontarf won again at Stratford-on-Avon, but Tim Molony drew level with a victory on Dramamine in the novices' 'chase at Uttoxeter on Whit-Saturday.

The season ended the following Monday, and normally, with so much at stake, Fred would probably have had at least four rides, which was actually Tim's total on the last vital day. It was Fred's old friend Halloween who unwittingly conspired to rob him of the chance of being champion for the second time.

Fred had again accepted a retainer to ride Halloween in all his races this year, and the Contessa's little horse was due to run in Hurst Park's big race on Whit-Monday, the Queen Elizabeth Chase. He also had five possible rides at Fontwell Park all with good chances, but he had no option but to go to Hurst Park.

While Tim Molony added two more to his own total at Towcester, Halloween, not a robust horse and one who had been giving his best throughout the season, ran unplaced behind the lightly-weighted Limb of the Law. So the final score was Tim Molony 67, Fred Winter 65, and the scene was set for another great battle the following season.

Before then, Diana Pearson had come back into Fred's life.

During Diana's world tour, Fred had had a couple of postcards from her, and after hearing that she was in hospital in Karachi with appendicitis at one stage, had had a frustrating telephone conversation with her, faint and broken by disconnections.

A fortnight before the Champion Hurdle Diana's mother had phoned him to say that Diana was returning home and would he like to go to the welcome home party. Fred went with mixed feelings. He wanted to see Diana again, but felt somehow that he had been neglected during the past 12 months by the girl to whom he had given every indication of his own feelings before she left.

The mood did not last long. He fell in love again with a crash and fortunately for him in the ensuing weeks Diana, who, in fairness, had hardly had much opportunity so far for assessing her own feelings about Fred, began to discover that she might just be in love with this stocky, tough individual with a serious face which could suddenly break into an infectious grin when something amused him.

They were engaged in April, and married the following May, by which time Fred was champion jockey. The wedding achieved more space in the papers than any event in Fred's career up to this point.

The most important happening for Fred during the current season – apart from his engagement to Diana – had been that he made the acquaintance of a horse who was to realise for him what had become one of his ambitions – to win the Grand National. The horse was the massive Sundew, whom he rode for the first time in the Welsh Grand National at Chepstow, finishing second to Monaleen in spite of breaking a blood vessel.

Sundew was the third horse that Mr and Mrs Geoffrey Kohn had bought in attempting to find a Grand National winner. First they purchased Quite Naturally, who fell at the first fence in the 1953 race, and then Churchtown, who ran extremely well to finish fourth to Royal Tan in 1954.

Sundew was bought for something under £3,000 after he had won three races in Ireland during the 1954–55 season and had run second to Copp in the Leopardstown Chase. This price, incidentally, reflects the amazing upward swing in the sort of money that has to be found by anyone wanting to buy a horse with Grand National potential. You now start at £6,000 for anything which has shown it can plod round in a long distance steeplechase in quite moderate company.

Sundew carried the Kohn colours in the 1955 National, ridden by Paddy Doyle, who had ridden him in most of his races in Ireland. He ran a fine race and was up with the leaders at the Canal Turn second time. Two fences later he made a mistake, and then came down at the 26th fence.

It was only 18 days later that Fred had his first ride on him. As he walked round the Chepstow parade ring Sundew looked exactly like a horse who had had a hard race at Aintree, lean and rather tired.

In spite of this he ran a good honest race, joining the leaders half a mile from home and being run out of it only after the last fence by Monaleen, who was carrying 9 st 7 lb and receiving 24 lb from Sundew. It was the start of a partnership between Fred and Sundew which had its ups and downs, but which resulted in tremendous triumph at Aintree.

Fred started the 1955–56 season with retainers to ride two good horses in all their races – Halloween and Sundew. They could not have been of greater contrast. Halloween was small, light-framed and built like a greyhound. Sundew was one of the biggest horses in training, measuring more than 17 hands.

Both were tremendously game, but when Fred finished second on Halloween behind Pointsman in the Cottage Rake Chase at Kempton Park in November, beaten only a short head, he was not to know that they would never win a race again together.

Halloween missed the King George VI Chase on Boxing Day because of a slight leg injury and then finished second again to Pointsman at Sandown Park in January, third in a handicap at Newbury under the enormous weight for him of 12 st 8 lb, and third to Limber Hill in the Cheltenham Gold Cup.

The following season, after two more outings, his heart began to deteriorate.

His trainer, Bill Wightman, was bending down in Halloween's box one day to examine a varicose vein which had swelled up in the horse's leg when he heard Halloween's

62

heart loud and clear, almost as if he was listening to it through a stethoscope.

The pulse was alarmingly irregular and Bill Wightman hardly needed confirmation from the vet that the gallant little horse, who had battled to the last ounce in finish after finish, was at the end of his racing career.

The last time he was seen in public was when he took part, at the age of 21, in a Parade of Champions, staged by Kempton Park on Boxing Day, 1966. He was accompanied by Peggy, a retired milk float pony who is still his inseparable companion at a home for retired horses at Lingfield in Surrey.

With Halloween on the sidelines for the King George VI Chase this season, Fred accepted the ride on Galloway Braes, who had been second to Halloween in that race in 1954 and had won it the year before, defeating Mont Tremblant.

Galloway Braes could be brilliant, and on firm ground he was also very fast. He is still the posthumous holder of the English record for a three miles steeplechase – 5 mins. 47.8 secs. – set up when he won the Queen Elizabeth II Chase at Hurst Park in 1953.

He was also one of the most frightening horses that a jockey could ride, for sometimes he forgot to jump a fence completely, and he had an alarming habit of diving at his fences.

Galloway Braes did nothing wrong in this race, and it was Fred who afterwards had to admit that their neck defeat by the massive Limber Hill from Yorkshire was his own fault :

We led all the way and jumped the last clear, and I made the unforgivable mistake of looking round. Not only did I do that, but I looked the wrong side. While I was looking to the left, Jimmy Power was coming up on the other side on Limber Hill. All I had to do was to keep my horse going on the run-in and he would have won. By the time I realised

63

what was happening, Limber Hill had got in front and I couldn't get Galloway Braes going again in time. For a man of my experience it was completely unforgivable.

The one rather wonderful thing that came out of it was that one of the press, Bob Butchers of the Daily Mirror, *came to me afterwards and showed me what he had written about the incident and said did I mind him publishing it. I think he must have been the only person on the racecourse who realised what a mess I had made of it; certainly he was the only person who mentioned it to me. I said I couldn't stop him printing it, though I obviously would be happier if he didn't, and when I looked at the paper the next day he had in fact left it out. I must say that the press as a whole were very kind to me, but I thought this was one of the nicest things anyone ever did for me in racing.*

Above: The Winter family—Diana and Fred, Denise, Philippa and Joanna. *Below:* The maddest of all ways of making a living. Fred did this 319 times

Heroes' welcome. Fred rides Sundew through the street of Henley-in-Arden two days after they had won the Grand National

CHAPTER SEVEN

SOME NATIONAL HORSE!

Fred's partnership with Sundew did not get off to an auspicious start when they teamed up for the first time in the 1955–56 season.

With Aintree in mind, Frank Hudson, who trained the big horse at Henley-in-Arden, not far from the Kohn's home, did not bring Sundew out until Newbury on the last day of the Old Year.

He looked magnificent as Fred cantered him to the start, and as he passed Diana and Ryan Price's wife, Dorothy, who were walking down to watch the race by the last fence, Fred shouted 'What do you think of my National horse?' 'Some National horse' they shouted a few minutes later as Fred sheepishly cantered Sundew back after they had fallen at the third fence.

But Fred was not at all dispirited. He was convinced that the fall had not been Sundew's fault. The ground was slippery, Sundew had jumped the fence perfectly and then lost his footing on landing. Fred was on his feet in a moment and caught the horse before he galloped off.

He still had great faith in him, and less than a fortnight later they won a three miles 'chase at Hurst Park comfortably. It was not the ideal track for this huge, long-striding horse, but Fred for once deserted the inside rail and let Sundew lope round on the outside, giving him a clear view of his fences all the way. He took the lead more than a mile from home and ran on to a three lengths win from the odds-on favourite Triplepatte.

The race must have helped to allay any loss of confidence that Sundew may have felt after his experience at Newbury, and he was probably a great deal better for the outing. He blew enormously in the unsaddling enclosure.

In his next race, the National Trial Chase over three and a half miles at Haydock Park, he led from start to finish and just held off the challenge of the previous year's Grand National winner, Quare Times.

Sundew had been right up with Quare Times when he fell in the National, so there was every reason for the stable to think that, given reasonable luck, the big horse had a great chance in this year's race.

Before going to Aintree, Sundew had one more outing, in the Hearts of Oak Chase at Manchester, and, in the sort of deep glue which this racecourse turned to after a lot of rain, he failed honourably to give six pounds to E.S.B., whose path was also leading to Aintree.

Fred went through the big Cheltenham meeting the following week without a winner, but he had been riding plenty of winners throughout the winter, and he was close behind Tim Molony in the championship table. He had two major goals for the last few weeks of the season – the Grand National and the N.H. Jockeys' Championship.

The atmosphere in the jockeys' room at Aintree before the Grand National was as brittle as ever. The size of the fences out there beyond the packed grandstand, the prize at stake, the mathematical fact that, certainly until the fences were made rather easier recently, less than a third of the field would complete the course safely – all these contribute to the tension.

National Hunt jockeys are a high-spirited bunch and in spite of, or perhaps because of, the dangers surrounding them even in the course of any ordinary day's racing at a small meeting, they fool around and pull each others legs in a way which makes their changing room seem like an uncontrolled fourth form class-room by comparison with the more serious atmosphere in which their flat racing colleagues go to work.

But at Aintree, jokes which might have been funny two days earlier at Taunton, raise only half smiles as everyone sits around in that last half hour before the official comes to the door and calls 'Jockeys out, please'.

Fred's record in steeplechases at Aintree as he sat waiting to join Mr and Mrs Kohn and Frank Hudson in the paddock at Aintree was two rides and two falls. Both falls had been in the Grand National, but this time he went out as hopeful as any jockey can be before a race such as this.

His horse was superbly fit. Sundew had won two of his last three races and was far from disgraced when he was beaten in his latest one. He had gone well for nearly four miles in the previous year's National, and Fred felt that he had really found the way to ride him :

He was the sort of horse you had to leave alone and let him run his own race. You couldn't pull him around. He had that enormous stride on him, and if you tried to pull him out of it, you got him completely unbalanced. Again, although he was tremendously large, he couldn't stand back at a fence. If you asked him to, he would just about make it, but it was far better to let him take another stride and fiddle over it on his own rather than give him a kick to make him take off early.

Fred knew all this when he rode out on Sundew. From the start he let him run on along with the leaders, jumping superbly all the way round the first circuit. Turning away from the stands to start the second circuit, he let Sundew go up into the lead with Armorial III, who had been in front from the second fence. Down the row of six fences in a straight line alongside the great railway bank, culminating in Becher's Brook, Sundew had one horse in front of him to bother about – Mariner's Log, who had fallen early and now, riderless and wearing blinkers, was weaving about the course getting in Fred's way.

Fred swore and coming to Becher's again he drove Sundew into the fence.

The loose horse had taken his mind off what he should or should not be doing on Sundew. It was a fatal error.

Instead of standing back to jump as Fred had asked him to, Sundew took another stride which put him right under the towering fence. He hit it on the way up and was completely bowled over, landing the other side on his head with a terrible crash.

Fred and Sundew were the only fallers at Becher's that year. The field swept by with a thudding and crashing, and it was Dave Dick who went on to win the race on E.S.B., after that incredible drama in which the Queen Mother's horse Devon Loch slipped up 30 yards from the post with the race safely won.

Fred rode back to the weighing room in an ambulance, unhurt but furious with himself for the lapse. It was an experience which was to bring positive results in the future.

There was still another battle to be won before the end of the season. Tim Molony had been at the top of the jockeys' table from quite early in the season but early in April it suddenly appeared that he was no certainty to be champion. Fred had moved up to only four behind him, a double at Cheltenham on April 12 put him two behind, and then wins at Wye and Wincanton placed him level with Tim.

Tim took the lead again, but by May 7 Fred was three in the lead, and five days later he was four ahead. The final score was 74 to 70 in Fred's favour. 'My wedding present to Fred,' said Tim at the end of the battle.

Two days after the end of the season, Fred and Diana were married in London. The note at the top of a page in one of Fred's newspaper cuttings books says 'Our Wedding – what a day, what a party'.

It was indeed a party, with almost every department of racing represented. Fred's brother John was best man and his brother-in-law Doug Smith, champion flat race jockey that year, supplied a bridesmaid and a page boy for the occasion in his daughter and son, Wendy and Michael. Tim Molony and many of the other jumping jockeys, owners, trainers, stewards, officials, were there.

After the wedding in St James's, Spanish Place, the reception went on for some hours. Some of the flat race jockeys had to make an early departure for an evening meeting at Alexandra Park (Doug Smith celebrated the occasion by riding two winners, so the champagne cannot have done him any harm), but not before the telegrams read out had included jockey Mick Dillon's contribution :

MAY YOUR SUMMERS TOGETHER BE BOTH HAPPY AND FINE
MAY YOUR WINTERS BE SHORT AND WEIGH SEVEN STONE NINE

which went down well with a gathering that included many who spent most of their lives battling against weight.

There have been no sons to carry on the Winter story in the saddle, but Fred and Diana have been rewarded with three delightful daughters, Denise, Joanna and Philippa, who spend most of their holidays riding their ponies, and most of their school terms thinking about them.

The home that Fred and Diana came back to after their honeymoon in France was Kitsbury Orchard, a house of Cotswold stone in a hollow on the outskirts of the village of Oddington, close to Stow-on-the-Wold. It was quiet, secluded, and had loose boxes and two paddocks for Diana's hunters and later the children's ponies. When Fred bought it after a long search lasting almost a year, the garden was a wilderness.

Fred and Diana worked hard through the summer, straightening out the place which was to be their home for the next eight years, and when they drove down to

Devonshire for the opening of the 1956–57 season at Buckfastleigh they felt they had made some real progress.

It was a good season for Fred, culminating in victory in the Grand National and his third jockeys' championship. Winners came thick and fast in the early weeks of the season. The longest he went without a winner throughout the season was 17 rides, and he escaped any serious injury – that is, if losing the top of a finger does not count as a serious injury.

It happened when he was riding Mr Jimmy McLean's cheerful little horse Gold Wire in his first race over hurdles at Sandown Park in November.

Gold Wire loved jumping from the start and in schooling had been tremendously bold. He went into the first hurdle at Sandown in front, stood right back and made a great leap which was so good that he turned over as he landed.

Fred rolled away, curled up in a ball with his hands clasped round his head, but as Gold Wire got to his feet he kicked his rider on the back of the head.

Fred's helmet came off. It had done its job and saved him from anything more than a cut at the back of the skull, but when Fred looked down he saw that most of the top of one finger had disappeared.

Ryan Price drove Fred to East Grinstead Hospital, where a doctor grafted some skin on to the finger to cover the stump of bone which was sticking out, but Fred was too eager to return to riding to give the graft a fair chance.

He was back in the saddle only 19 days later, and though he had the finger well padded, the grafted portion went dead, and he was left with an unsightly mess.

A surgeon he consulted in Oxford told him that he could ride through the rest of the season with the finger covered with a stall and return when he felt like it to have the job tidied up. So after the Grand National Fred decided to take a fortnight off, went back to Oxford and lay on a couch while the surgeon gave his finger a local anaesthetic. The surplus bone was sawn off and the end of the shortened

70

finger neatly stitched up. It never gave Fred any further trouble.

Diana was by now well aware of some of the anxieties of being married to a National Hunt jockey – what it was like to watch from the grandstand or on television as Fred disappeared in a turmoil of flying birch and falling horse, or failed to return with the other runners from the far end of the course on a murky November day.

Herself a capable rider to hounds, Diana appeared on the surface to worry less about the prospects of Fred actually falling than about the after effects once it had happened.

'Before the National, or, in fact, any big race,' she said, 'I used to get very nervous, but more because I wanted Fred to win than anything else. Anyway, Fred always used to say that you never get very bad falls in the National compared to hurdle races and two miles steeplechases.

'What worried me most was him having a fall and then driving back from a meeting. He had a fall at Leicester once and he passed out when he got home. He could so easily have done it while he was driving. Again, you always seemed to come back from meetings in the worst possible driving light. That, I think, is one of the toughest aspects of going racing. National Hunt jockeys don't have chauffeurs.

'Fred never complained about the injuries, though, and because he never really bruised so that it showed, I think he suffered more than he said. He was a very good patient, very relaxed, and he probably got better quicker than most people.'

Diana, now expecting her first baby, was watching television at home on Boxing Day when Fred had what was his second ride, and his last, on Galloway Braes. This was in the King George VI Chase, in which they had been so narrowly beaten by Limber Hill 12 months ago.

Winners were coming thick and fast for Fred, but his ride on Galloway Braes was to end in tragedy. Perhaps it was fortunate for Diana that the TV cameras were not on

Galloway Braes when he almost failed to take off at the last open ditch. He crashed to the ground, knocking out Fred, and shattering his own near foreleg.

As the winner Rose Park returned to the unsaddling enclosure after beating the Queen Mother's luckless Grand National runner of the previous season, Devon Loch, the Kempton Park vet was driven out through the mist to the fence where Galloway Braes had fallen. He had no option but to use the humane killer.

Fred himself soon recovered from the fall. The following day at Newbury he rode the winner of the first race, Cortego, and completed a double in the fourth with Retour de Flamme.

Staying with Fred and Diana was an American, Dudley Fort, an amusing extrovert with a comment for every occasion. He was in the middle of a hunting holiday in England and Ireland, during which he managed to have an incredible number of days in the field with many different packs and saw some racing as well.

On the way back to Kitsbury from Newbury races, they called at Oxford where Diana was due to see the gynaecologist for a check up. After he had examined her, the doctor informed Diana that she was going to have twins, which prompted the remark from Dudley Fort 'Gee, what a day. A double in the afternoon and a double in the evening. What a guy you are, Winter.'

'Uncle Dudley,' as he is known to many horsemen in and around Nashville, Tennessee, as well as on this side of the Atlantic, had returned to America by the time the twins arrived. On February 4, a day when Fred was to have his first ride on the popular Crudwell in a steeplechase at Warwick, Diana was rushed to the Radcliffe Infirmary for the premature birth of two girls by a Caeserean operation. They weighed 5 lb 4 oz and 4 lb 10 oz.

Fred changed rapidly after his successful ride on Crudwell and tore back to Oxford, to wait until eight o'clock in the

All the power and determination of a Winter finish as Fred drives
Doxford into the last hurdle at Newbury

Above: Fred turns to canter Fare Time to the start before the 1959 Champion Hurdle – the second of the three Champions that he won. *Below:* 'I never thought we would stay in front all the way up the hill'. A tiring Saffron Tartan jumps the last fence in the 1961 Gold Cup well clear of Pas Seul. He won by a length and a half

evening before hearing that Diana and the twins, had come through a difficult time in safety.

Though Fred was riding a high percentage of winners at this time, the big Cheltenham meeting in March saw him in the middle of his longest losing run of the season, and he suffered disappointment after disappointment.

Clair Soleil had won four of his six previous races and had put up a brilliant performance in winning the Rose of Lancaster Hurdle at Manchester in very heavy going.

He now started favourite for the Champion Hurdle but ran well below his best form and finished unplaced behind Merry Deal. The nearest Fred came to winning at Cheltenham was when he finished a five lengths second on Cortego in the Gloucestershire Hurdle division that Dave Dick won on Tokoroa.

Sundew went to Aintree in great heart. He had given Fred a superb ride in his previous race, the Grand International Chase at Sandown Park, leading from start to finish and jumping brilliantly, but on his Aintree form alone, the signs were not auspicious.

He had fallen in the two previous Grand Nationals, and in November of this season he gave a deplorable show of jumping in the Grand Sefton Chase there. He hit fence after fence and at the jump after Becher's, Fred found himself with both feet on the off side of the saddle, only managing to untangle himself seconds before they came to the Canal Turn fence.

The Sandown win had raised Fred's hopes again, and before the National Frank Hudson had had the big horse driven south from Henley-in-Arden to Berkshire to do his final gallop. Over a testing, uphill mile and a quarter on the Faringdon Road gallops at Childrey, Sundew beat Poise and War King, two greys with winning form, out of sight.

Fred's thoughts had been continually on the Grand

National as he drove to and from meetings in the weeks before the big race. In the past, jockeys had told him that the only way to ride Aintree was to kick, kick, all the time, but his experience to date, and particularly with Sundew, had suggested that this was the last thing he should do on March 29.

I had watched the master of all at Liverpool, Pat Taaffe, as much as I possibly could. Going into a fence he hardly moved. In fact, rather than kick them into a fence, Pat was inclined to check them, pull them back on their hocks and let them pop over. I remember reading an article in which Pat said that he himself was taught by Dan Moore who said to him that at Liverpool you want to hunt and hunt and hunt until you come on to the racecourse, and then you can start thinking about being a jockey. I am absolutely convinced this is right.

At Wincanton, before going to Aintree, Fred had talked to Dudley Williams, who was twice placed in the National and won the race on Kellsboro' Jack in 1933. He asked him for his opinion of the best way round Aintree. Dudley Williams' route is virtually the one which Fred followed in all his subsequent races at Liverpool, jumping about the middle of the left half of each fence the whole way round.

Fred found that as most jockeys tended to keep away from the part of the fence nearest the inside rail because the drop on the landing side there is slightly greater, he was freer from interference from other horses.

Grand National day, cold, misty and rainy, did not start off well, for Fred was beaten into third place on the 9 to 4 favourite Cortego in the Coronation Hurdle. It was another of the few occasions on which Fred received a real dressing down from Ryan Price.

The trainer's instructions had been to keep Cortego well up among the leaders and make plenty of use of him on this sharp hurdles course. In the event, Fred was slow away from the start and, in a fast-run race, was always struggling to make up ground.

Cortego was flying at the finish, but it was too late, and Ryan Price expressed himself in no uncertain terms as Fred rode back.

Eleven horses out of 35 starters completed the course in the National, for which Neville Crump provided both the favourite in Goosander, winner of the Haydock Park National Trial Chase, and second favourite, Much Obliged.

The long-striding Armorial III, who had led for much of the way the previous year, set off in front again, but he came down at the fourth fence, and from that point Sundew was the leader for all but a few strides on the second circuit.

We went like hell from the start, as they always do, but you couldn't pull Sundew about so I just let him stride on in his own time. After Armorial III fell, I never saw another soul until we were going out into the country for the second time and then Derek Ancil came up almost alongside on Colonel Whitbread's horse, Athenian. He kept me company for half a dozen fences, and I shouted across to Derek go steady, because we were going much too fast. Luckily he did, which gave both horses a bit of a breather. Sundew was a bit lucky at Becher's second time, because he pitched on landing, but he recovered and then we started to leave Athenian behind.

Coming on to the racecourse, Dave Dick appeared for a moment on E.S.B. and he seemed to be going much too well. In fact he was grinning all over his face and shouted I would have to get a move on if I was going to win, but then E.S.B. started to weaken. Even so, Sundew was terribly tired and I shall never forget jumping the last and looking at that long run-in. I was thinking Oh my God, we will be in the first three but we certainly can't win, he's so tired. He literally felt as though he was going up and down on the same spot.

75

But miraculously nothing got to us, and in the end we won eight lengths from Wyndburgh.

So for the first time Fred experienced a hero's welcome at Aintree. He was interviewed in a crowded press room ('Mr Winter, what happened to make you fall off last year,' asked a young lady from a Sunday paper).

There was a party afterwards given by Sundew's owners, Mr and Mrs Kohn, at the Prince of Wales Hotel, Southport. The rapidly printed menu, bearing the Kohn colours, included Asperges Winter au Beurre Fondue and Corbeille des Roses Sundew.

The following Monday, Fred and Sundew paraded through the streets of Henley-in-Arden, and with trainer Frank Hudson and the owners were congratulated by the High Bailiff of the Court Leet, who also presented Mrs Kohn with a parchment scroll commemorating the victory of a courageous horse and a great jockey.

After these exertions, it was decided to run Sundew again in the inaugural Whitbread Gold Cup at Sandown Park on April 27 – a decision which Fred fought tooth and nail because he felt Sundew had done enough for the season. He lost the argument and Sundew went to Sandown. He made several mistakes in the early part of the race, and Fred pulled him up after he had jumped 20 fences without showing any hope of getting into the front rank.

Sundew ran only three more races in his life. Early in the next season he had an outing in a hurdle race at Nottingham, finishing third. At Liverpool's Autumn meeting, he completed the course in the Grand Sefton Chase, but jumped appallingly, as he had in that race 12 months earlier. Then on November 27, 1957, the big horse met his death.

Fred was needed to ride Feluma, a winner for the Price stable at Windsor, and Derek Leslie was asked to ride Sundew at Haydock in a three miles 'chase. Sundew blundered at the water jump in front of the stands. Two other horses cannoned into him as he scrambled out of the water. Derek Leslie was unshipped and Sundew cantered on for 200 yards to pull up by the gate into the paddock, obviously badly injured. He had smashed a bone in the shoulder.

Sundew was loaded into a float and driven back to the racecourse stables where, apparently in no great pain, he enjoyed a hot mash prepared by his stable lad Geoff Gibson, while his own vet, Mr Norman Gold of Redditch, drove the 110 miles north to Haydock Park. Mr Gold had to take the awful decision that Sundew's chances of surviving the injury were slender, and five hours after the accident the big horse was destroyed. He is buried on the racecourse close to the grave of another famous steeplechaser, Fly Mask, who also met his death at Haydock Park.

I think it is very sad that a horse who has jumped all those big fences going two thirds of the way round Liverpool twice in the National, completed the course in two Grand Seftons, and won a National, should do himself in at a water jump. The only thing is – and it may sound hard – you at least know where they are when they have been put to sleep. You know they are not wandering on getting more and more miserable like a lot of horses do when they are retired after being in training for years.

CHAPTER EIGHT

HIS GREATEST SEASON?

By the time that Sundew was killed, Fred had won the 1956–57 jockeys' championship with 80 victories, 22 more than his nearest rival, Michael Scudamore, and was heading for the championship for the fourth time.

He won the first race of the season at Newton Abbot on Happy Mullet, trained by Ryan Price, reached his half century with a double on the same stable's St Stephen and Malacca III at Nottingham on January 29, and finished 23 wins ahead of Tim Brookshaw with a total of 82 when Record Breaker won at Southwell on April 28.

Turning through the pages of the newspapers of this period, one is inclined to ask 'Was this his greatest season?' Day after day there were headlines featuring great efforts by Fred. His win on Pouding in a long distance hurdle at Sandown Park in January was undoubtedly one of the best rides of his career.

The *Sporting Life*'s Tom Nickalls wrote in the next day's paper : 'I feel sorry for anyone who has to ride a finish against this inexorable and superlative performer, for it seems, no matter what you do, Fred Winter's horse gets there just in front.'

Fred had ridden a brilliant race throughout on Pouding, sitting as firm as rock when the horse made a mistake at the fourth-last hurdle. Halfway up the run-in Pouding, involved in his third hard finish in a month, showed signs of giving up the struggle, but Fred drove him home with all the power he could muster to beat Dandy Scot, receiving over two stone, by a short head.

78

Pouding's trainer Fulke Walwyn would not have been totally unbiased in this moment of triumph when he said, 'I think Fred is the greatest I have ever seen,' but another who saw the race was L. B. Rees, brother of the great F. R. (Dick) Rees, five times champion jockey in the 1920's. He commented: 'Dick couldn't have done it any better, even at the height of his form.'

Fred did not win a single big race during this great season, but he was never out of the news.

His win on Taxidermist at Ludlow in October was the 500th of his jumping career. At Sandown in November he rode his brother John's second runner since taking out a licence to train jumpers for Mr Percy Bartholomew. This was Gads Hill and it was a great moment for the Winter family as Fred rode back to the unsaddling enclosure after Gads Hill had won by three lengths.

This was a marvellous start for Johnny, but I must say that I have never particularly liked riding for the family. So much seems to depend on the result that it gets one in a state of nerves before the start. It is much easier if you don't really know the connections of the horse. Then it doesn't matter to you personally *whether the horse gets beat or not – you just ride the race impassionately and as best you can.*

In the same way, I was never what you might call a gambling trainer's jockey. I always had a horror of people losing money because of me, and I think if you ride a horse for people knowing they have had a hell of a bet on him, it definitely upsets you. You are inclined to be over-anxious and to do the wrong thing instead of being relaxed. That's how it affected me, anyway.

Champion hurdler Clair Soleil won first time out over fences at Warwick this season, but he hated steeplechasing and it was not until he was put back to hurdles that he won again. By this time he was ten years old and never again achieved the brilliance he had shown in the 1955 Champion Hurdle.

Probably the best horse, or at least the most promising, that Fred rode over fences this season was Mr Gerry Judd's French-bred Le Palatin, who had proved himself a good handicap hurdler and now became brilliant over fences.

Le Palatin had a tremendous turn of acceleration which allowed Fred to wait to the last moment to challenge. He did this at Lingfield Park in December, beating the well fancied Limeville from the last jump. Le Palatin defeated the Queen Mother's Double Star in much the same way in the Henry VIII Chase at Hurst Park, won another race on the same course and Fred was looking forward to riding him in the best company the following season when this potentially top class 'chaser was killed outright in a race at Newbury.

Fred had a retainer this season for Mr H. J. Joel, whose jumpers were trained by Bobby Renton in Yorkshire. It was not a successful alliance, largely because of the great distance between Fred's home in Gloucestershire and the Renton stables in Yorkshire. Fred did win a novices' 'chase at Cheltenham in October on Mr Joel's Caesar's Helm, as well as the Mildmay of Flete Challenge Cup on the same course in March, but these were the only victories from a retainer which involved him in less than a dozen rides.

At Liverpool in March, Fred had an enjoyable ride on Roughan in the 2¾m. Topham Trophy Chase. Roughan's win prompted Fred to remark again that some of the Northern trainers, notably Bobby Renton and Roughan's trainer, that ebullient, red-faced and forthright Neville Crump ('Tell that —— policeman to move over and let some of the cars out of this dunghill of a car park') produced some of the best schooled horses in the country.

The horse that drew the greatest admiration from Fred this season, however, was Done Up.

Owned by Mr John Baillie and trained by Ryan Price, he

was probably the laziest horse ever to go into training. Fred won three novices' 'chases on him and then a handicap at Sandown Park, and it was always a case of kick, kick, drive, the whole way through a race.

If you look back at the comments in *Chaseform* on Done Up's races you will find time and again 'hard driven from 9th', 'hard driven throughout', 'made all, driven along from last', and so on.

I hate hitting a horse, but Done Up was a real crippler and unless you kept at him the whole time, he was useless. The only chance you got of having a breather was to give him a crack with the whip and he would go for about a hundred yards while you got your breath back. I will never forget when Harry Sprague won the Whitbread Gold Cup on him – his very last ride before he retired and when I was out with a skull injury. Harry was a great hurdles jockey and didn't usually ride over fences, but he was terribly strong. He had to drive Done Up the whole way and he beat Mandarin a short head, and on the way back to unsaddle through the members' enclosure, Harry was sick. He literally vomited through exhaustion. That's how tough horses can be.

Fred ended the season with 82 winning rides. He went out on to the course 359 times, and he fell 17 times. His winning percentage of 22.84 was higher than that of any other leading jockey, and though history was yet to be written and many a fine finish ridden, this was the season when Fred Winter was seen as the jockey complete – adaptable to many types of horse, fair to his oponents throughout a race, courageous as he drove a tiring horse into the last fence, and seldom beaten in a hard finish.

As the season got into its stride, the Winter team at home was strengthened by the arrival of another daughter, Philippa, born on October 24.

It was the last season in which Fred was champion jockey, though by no means the last in which he was one of the most powerful forces in National Hunt racing.

At the start of the 1958–59 season he accepted a retainer to ride all the horses that Ivor Herbert trained in the Chilterns for Mr Michael Sobell, the television magnate.

Among them was Flame Gun who had won three races in Ireland and now made his debut in England at Birmingham on November 5. He quickly raised Fred's hopes for the future by cantering home to an easy win from the favourite, Wayward Bird.

Fred had made a slow start to the season, and Tim Brookshaw had raced ahead with 22 winners more than the champion by the end of September, but Fred knew for certain that Flame Gun was going to be at least one useful contributor to his total in the months ahead.

Living up to his promise, Flame Gun won a novices' 'chase at Sandown next, and then at Newbury late in November Fred had to ride Staghound, a handsome grey trained by Ryan Price, in a novices' 'chase for which Flame Gun started favourite. Con McCormack, attached to Flame Gun's stable and claiming the three pounds allowance, rode Mr Sobell's horse, and came through with flying colours, taking the lead two fences from home and going on to beat Fred and Staghound by three lengths. But at Hurst Park less than a month later, the position was reversed. It was one of the most thrilling races ever to take place between two really fast two mile 'chasers.

Staghound and Flame Gun drew right away from the rest of the field, and coming to the last fence it looked as though Flame Gun was going just the better, for Fred had shown the whip to Staghound a furlong earlier.

As they approached the fence, Fred drove Staghound into it and the grey accelerated to fly over and land so fast that he stumbled. But Staghound's sudden acceleration had also upset Flame Gun, and while Staghound picked himself up on landing, Flame Gun hit the top of the fence and came down, leaving Staghound to win by a distance.

It was a classic case of tactics deciding an issue which was absolutely in the balance until that last jump. Fred said afterwards he had never before gone into any fence as fast as he did on Staghound.

Fred resumed his alliance with the horse he had succeeded in putting on the floor at Hurst Park three months later at the big Cheltenham meeting, when Flame Gun landed the Cotswold Chase beating the heavily backed Irish horse Cashel View, and earning from Fred the testimonial of 'the best two mile 'chaser I have ever ridden'. Flame Gun rounded off the season by winning the Champion Novice Chase at Manchester.

His win at Cheltenham was the first of five for Fred.

Fare Time, who had fallen at the first hurdle the year before, did nothing wrong in the Champion Hurdle and ran on gallantly under terrific driving from Fred from half a mile out to beat a very game mare called Ivy Green, giving Fred and Ryan Price their second triumph in this race. The same day, Fred won the Grand Annual Challenge Cup on Top Twenty, trained in Ireland by Clem Magnier.

After three wins on the first day of the meeting, Fred had no luck on the second day. The nearest he came to victory was when Top Twenty, saddled again less than 24 hours after winning, ran a gallant but hopeless second against the brilliant Quita Que in the Champion Chase, but Fred was back in form on the third day of the meeting.

Clair Soleil, Ryan Price's champion hurdler of three seasons earlier, was still going strong at the age of 10 and winning races wherever stamina and ability to act in heavy going counted. He had won the Victory Hurdle in bottomless going at Manchester, and now Fred rode a superbly judged race on him in the Spa Hurdle over three miles.

He showed all the judgment of pace of a Scobie Breasley in leading every inch of the way, and had enough up his sleeve coming to the final uphill three hundred yards to hold off all challengers. Half an hour later Fred went out on Gallery Goddess from the Flame Gun stable and got this mare home by a hard fought half length in the Grand Annual Challenge Cup.

Linwell, the Gold Cup winner of two seasons earlier, was Fred's mount in the big race, but any chance he had disappeared completely in the last fence shemozzle created by that superb but erratic horse Pas Seul. Linwell was lying second to Pas Seul as they came to the last, and Pas Seul, perhaps taking too much interest in the crowd, completely ignored the existence of the jump. He fell almost in Linwell's path, and also nearly brought down the Queen Mother's horse Lochroe who was following.

Fred on Linwell had to snatch up everything and steer round Pas Seul, while the Irish horse Roddy Owen, finding a clear path on the inside, went through into the lead and beat Linwell three lengths. There is little doubt that Pas Seul would have been the winner and Linwell would have had to be content with second place in any case.

If you ask Fred Winter what is the best horse he ever rode, he will, on reflection, give you not one of the horses with which his name was so often linked – Mandarin, Saffron Tartan, Clair Soleil or Fare Time – but Pas Seul.

Their partnership was brief for Fred rode Mr John Rogerson's horse just once, in a two miles 'chase at Stratford in 1961. The distance was short enough for Pas Seul, but his trainer, Bob Turnell, was sharpening him up for a tilt at the Whitbread Gold Cup a fortnight later, and Fred enjoyed Pas Seul's jumping at its best, winning a comfortable eight lengths from the useful Blue Dolphin.

In the Whitbread that year, Fred was riding Mandarin, and Dave Dick had the ride on Pas Seul, who by this stage in his career had won the 1960 Cheltenham Gold Cup and been beaten by Saffron Tartan in the 1961 race after being seriously off colour shortly before the race.

The 1961 Whitbread Gold Cup is probably the race which confirmed in Fred's mind, and that of many others, that Pas Seul at his best was one of the best steeplechasers we have seen since the war. He carried top weight of 12 stone to a brilliant win from the Grand National winner Nicolaus Silver, finishing as if he was ready to go round again. Fred's view of this win was from some 16 lengths further back on Mandarin, who was receiving four pounds from Pas Seul.

Ryan Price's objective for Done Up this season was the Grand National. Mr Baillie's horse won a race at Hurst Park in December and then, at Kempton Park in February, shattered everyone's confidence by falling at the last fence in a three-horse race. Fred remounted him to finish second to the 20 to 1 outsider Stanton Johnnie, and next time out Done Up won the National Trial Chase at Hurst Park.

But at Aintree they were brought down at Becher's first time round. After two races the following season this tough horse broke down, never to race again.

Fred looked all set for his fifth jockeys' championship at the start of April 1959, but then on the fourth day of the month he had a bad fall at Leicester riding the novice 'chaser Charles Brandon. He was severely concussed, and an X-ray showed that he had fractured his skull.

Tim Brookshaw, his nearest rival in the jockeys' table, slipped by into the lead and with Fred out of action for the rest of the season, Tim, who later was to show great courage in overcoming the effects of paralysis below the waist sustained in a fall at Aintree, finished the battle with 83 winning rides to Fred's 74.

Fred returned to the fray fit and well at the start of the new season. For the record he had now been involved in 227 falls, hitting the ground at speeds never much less than 30 m.p.h., amidst a flurry of rolling horses. He was on the floor 29 times during the 1959–60 season, or roughly once a week, but it was a good season and he completely escaped injury.

85

Ryan Price introduced Fred to a promising new horse when he went down to Findon in August. This was Eborneezer, who won his only two races over hurdles and, by landing the Grey Talk Hurdle at Hurst Park in March, somewhat made up for the disappointment that Fare Time, now owned by the Contessa di Saint' Elia, had suffered a leg injury and could not go for his second Champion Hurdle.

At Windsor in December, Fred had a brief renewal of his partnership with Mandarin, whose usual rider Gerry Madden was out of action. It was Mandarin's last race before the King George VI Chase, for which he was favourite. Fred had not ridden Mandarin since early in 1956, when he had won a long distance hurdle on him at Sandown Park at the age of five. He had also finished third on him in a similar race at Ludlow that season, and Fred remembered well Mandarin's determination in both races to shake off, if he could, any horse that tried to come alongside him.

By the time he rode him again at Windsor, Mandarin had already won 11 races and Mme. Hennessy's little horse had thousands of followers who had been desperately disappointed to see him beaten a short head by Done Up in the previous season's Whitbread Gold Cup.

Mandarin started at 6 to 1 on for his Windsor outing, and Fred felt, as deputing rider, that he personally was 'on a hiding to nothing'. It was just a question of getting Mandarin round safely, but in those days he was not the best of rides.

'Not jump well,' was the comment in *Chaseform* on the Windsor race, but he negotiated the 18 fences and won easily. Mandarin duly won the King George VI Chase, with Gerry Madden back in the saddle, beating Pointsman by a head. Pas Seul had one of his days when his jumping would have been a disgrace if perpetrated by a complete novice and he finished 15 lengths further back.

Fred was fourth on Flame Gun, whose effort seemed to confirm that, brilliant though he could be at two miles and even two and a half miles, he did not truly stay three miles in top class company.

Two seasons were to go by before Fred sat on Mandarin again, but looking to the immediate future at this stage he now had two horses which he could be fairly certain would carry him well in the best class in their particular spheres.

When Eborneezer won the Grey Talk Hurdle at Hurst Park in March, Ryan Price put him away until the following season feeling confident that it would take a good one to beat him in the following season's Champion Hurdle. Then at Cheltenham in April, Fred was asked to ride for the first time Saffron Tartan, owned in partnership by Lady Cottenham, Colonel Guy Westmacott and Captain R. Westmacott. Saffron Tartan, trained for them by Don Butchers (himself an intrepid rider over fences, somewhat similar in style to Fred), had been bought from Vincent O'Brien's stable in Ireland, and had so far won six races. He proved an expensive failure in the 1959 Whitbread Gold Cup which Done Up won from Mandarin, starting at the short price of 5 to 2 and finishing well down the field under top weight.

He then went to Don Butchers' stables at Epsom and after winning the Champion Trial Hurdle at Birmingham, he ran third to Another Flash in the big race itself at Cheltenham — a fair effort for a nine-year-old who really needed something more than two miles to produce the best in him.

Fred teamed up with Saffron Tartan at Cheltenham when this strong, imposing horse had his first race over fences for some time. It was a thrilling experience for Fred. Saffron Tartan jumped brilliantly, took the lead under his 12 st 7 lb before the third fence from home, and won unextended by five lengths.

This was Fred's 58th winner of the season. Four days later he achieved the 700th win of his career on Prince at Uttoxeter, and he won seven more races before the end of the season. But it was not enough. By May 2 Fred was six wins ahead of Stan Mellor. The gap closed slowly until with two days to go, the score was Winter 67, Mellor 66.

Both riders went to Midlands racecourses on the pen-ultimate day and both rode a winner – Fred at Towcester and Stan Mellor at Uttoxeter. But Fred had decided to call it a day and to go on holiday. He left on the midnight train from Paddington to join Diana and the children in Cornwall. Stan rode on the last day at Uttoxeter and while Fred was relaxing on a beach, Stan collected two more winners to land the title for the first time.

An enormously improved rider, Stan was to win the championship for three consecutive years, and his total for the following season was only four short of the record 121 set up by Fred in the 1952–53 season.

What will a season bring? So many times, a stable sets out at the start of a season with its yard apparently brimming with potential winners, and with its sights set on all the big races. Then things start to go wrong, horses break down, and one by one the hopes fade.

But for Fred in the 1960–61 season nearly all his dreams came true. Not only did Saffron Tarton and Eborneezer achieve their major objectives, but a new star appeared on the horizon in the shape of Cantab, a three-year-old bought in France by Ryan Price for dress designer Miss Edith Chanelle.

The story of this season culminates in a fantastic five days, from March 7 to March 11, when Fred won the feature race each day both at the big Cheltenham meeting and at Hurst Park.

It was not roses all the way to this week of triumph.

Saffron Tartan had his first outing in mid-October in the Grand Sefton Trial Chase at Hurst Park, and Fred, who now had a retainer to ride him in all his races, was not un-satisfied that he just failed to give a stone to Colonel Billy

Above: Half a length down at the last fence, Mandarin battled on under Fred's driving to beat Fortria (Pat Taaffe, left) by a length in the 1962 Gold Cup. *Below:* Safely over the last fence in the 1962 Grand National, Kilmore heads for the winning post in front of Mr What (left), who was second, Gay Navaree, fourth and Wyndburgh (right), third

Seconds after the Auteuil announcer had given the result of the 1962 Grand Steeplechase de Paris everyone looked happy. With Mandarin, broken bit dangling, are his lad 'Mush' Foster, owner Mme Peggy Hennessy and Fulke Walwyn's travelling head lad, the late 'Darkie' Leatham

Whitbread's good young horse Mariner's Dance. It was perhaps a harder race first time out than he would have liked for a horse who had ahead of him a stern programme involving the King George VI Chase and the Gold Cup.

Then came a switch back to two miles and a disappointing performance from Saffron Tartan in the Mackeson Gold Cup at Cheltenham. The big horse shared top weight with the Irishman Fortria, and on good going they went a tremendous gallop.

Saffron Tartan was beginning to make up some ground on the leaders four fences from home when he made one of his rare jumping mistakes. It was not a bad blunder but it meant that at that moment just before the pace always increases at Cheltenham, Saffron Tartan lost some ground. Fred did not get him back in the race, and they trailed in a long way behind the winner, Fortria.

There was gloom and despondency in the Saffron Tartan camp and a feeling that perhaps if Fred had persevered after that blunder the nine-year-old would have got back into the battle.

But Fred was thinking of the future and he had taken the decision that he would have been asking Saffron Tartan an impossible task which could have seriously penalised him in his big races to come.

Saffron Tartan went to Kempton Park on Boxing Day with something of a reputation as a 'talking horse'. He had now won eight races, but he had never made it in a big race, though he had been heavily backed a number of times.

Don Butchers had him looking magnificent, and the huge holiday crowd made him favourite again in front of the Hennessy Gold Cup winner Knucklecracker and King, a good two miler who was now having his attention turned to longer distances. After two miles Saffron Tartan was ahead of King, with Knucklecracker beginning to make his way through the field.

When Fred glanced over his shoulder as they came to the

last bend he realised that King was a real danger, but though Dave Dick's mount ran on gamely and showed beyond any shadow of doubt that he stayed three miles, Saffron Tartan quickened on the run-in and won by three lengths.

Don Butchers had decided to give Saffron Tartan just one race more before the Cheltenham Gold Cup, and he chose the Gainsborough Chase at Sandown Park in mid-February.

The event did nothing to inspire Saffron Tartan's supporters. After jumping the first seven fences brilliantly, he turned over on putting his foot in a slight hole after the eighth fence.

The roar of dismay from the crowd must have been heard miles away, and those who were trying to decide whether Saffron Tartan could complete the King George VI – Gold Cup double were left with no further evidence on which to assess his chances.

The paths of both Eborneezer and Cantab to that exciting Cheltenham – Hurst Park week in March also took in this day at Sandown Park, and in their cases all went well.

Cantab had won three consecutive races, though not against particularly strong opposition, but now he conceded weight to a number of useful juveniles and he won again. Ryan Price decided not to run him again before the Triumph Hurdle.

Eborneezer had not seen a racecourse since he won the Grey Talk Hurdle 11 months before, and it was not surprising that he was allowed to start at 6 to 1 for the Oteley Hurdle, a race which has often been a good trial for the Champion Hurdle.

Fred, who half an hour earlier had had his second win of the day on Pouding in the feature race, the Stone's Ginger Wine Chase, drove Eborneezer up to the leader and favourite, Morning Coat, as they came to the last hurdle and won by a length.

But the stable's hopes of victory in the Champion Hurdle were somewhat dampened when Eborneezer surprisingly failed to give four pounds to the useful but not top class Costa Brava in the Champion Hurdle Trial at Birmingham.

There was even talk of scratching Eborneezer from the Champion Hurdle, but Fred assured Ryan Price that the trouble lay in the poor pace at which the race was run. They had gone very fast only for the last half mile or so, and this was all against Eborneezer, who did not have a great turn of speed.

So the scene was set for Fred's triumphant week in March. He went to Cheltenham and Hurst Park reasonably confident of Saffron Tartan, hopeful about Eborneezer, optimistic about Cantab and with a good chance of finding a winner or two among the other horses he had been engaged for during the week.

His first win came on Ravencroft, trained by Fulke Walwyn for Mr Christopher Loyd, in the National Hunt Handicap Chase on the first day of Cheltenham. The crowd were treated to a great battle between Fred and Stan Mellor on Chavara.

Their horses drew away from the rest of the field and came to the last fence together, with Chavara, conceding a lot of weight to Ravencroft, only weakening and losing second place to the grey Owen's Sedge, on the run-in.

On the second day, the Champion Hurdle went for the third time in seven years to Ryan Price and Fred Winter, and though this was one of the most argued-about championships for many years, it cannot be taken away from Eborneezer that, in only his fifth race over hurdles, he jumped safely round to beat the best hurdlers that England and Ireland could produce.

The controversy arose from a pile-up two hurdles from home when the Irish horse Albergo rushed up to the leaders, going like a winner, and promptly fell, bringing down Birinkiana, Tonnerre de Brest and Morning Coat (whose rider, Derek Ancil, was also feeling hopeful of his chances).

Fred, who had had Eborneezer in the leading group the

whole way had been following his customary route on the
inner rail and missed all the trouble. Eborneezer took the
lead, leaving behind him a struggling mass of horses and
jockeys on the ground, and ran on to beat the fast finishing
Irish favourite Moss Bank by three lengths.

Eborneezer may have been lucky, but he looked a fresh
horse as he finished and could probably have pulled out
more. As John Lawrence wrote in the following day's *Daily
Telegraph* 'Eborneezer surely deserved the prize – the
obstacles, after all, are put there to be jumped'.

And then the Gold Cup the following day.

It was a good field, including last year's winner Pas Seul,
little Mandarin, a promising young horse in Frenchman's
Cove, King, and Knucklecracker.

There had been a great temptation to run Saffron Tartan
again in the Manifesto Chase at Lingfield Park following
his Sandown fall, but Fred begged Don Butchers to take
him out of the race :

*They were dying to run him, but the ground was ghastly.
There had been a lot of rain and it was as deep as Lingfield
can get. I made Don Butchers walk the course with me to
prove how bad it was, and I pleaded and pleaded with him
that he should convince the owners not to run the horse,
because I was certain it would tear the heart out of him.
After a hell of a lot of talk, they decided not to run. I think
if they had decided to, he would never even have seen
Cheltenham, let alone won.*

In spite of all the talent in the Gold Cup, the race
developed as many people hoped it would, into a tremendous
battle between Pas Seul and Saffron Tartan, and these two
dominated the race from the moment the field turned down
the hill approaching the third fence from home.

In brilliant sunshine, Fred set Saffron Tartan on his way
home with Pas Seul almost alongside. As they came to the

second last fence, Fred had hardly moved on Saffron Tartan, but Dave Dick was driving Pas Seul as hard as he could.

Between the last two fences, Saffron Tartan drew ahead and surely now the drama was all over. But suddenly Fred felt Saffron Tartan falter beneath him – his stamina was giving out.

Fred drew his whip and drove Saffron Tartan towards the last fence and on up the hill to the winning post. The race was decided at that last fence. Saffron Tartan jumped perfectly, while Pas Seul made a fatal blunder which checked him in his run.

Though Pas Seul was catching the leader again in the last hundred yards, Fred kept Saffron Tartan going to win by a length and a half, with Mandarin, finishing the fastest of them all, three lengths away in third place.

Never was Fred more glad to reach the winning post:

Before we got to the final jump, my horse was in a state of physical collapse, and I never thought we would stay in front all the way up the hill. The truth is that he never really stayed three and a quarter miles, and a stride after passing the winning post he was down to a walk, a very, very tired horse. I, too, was completely exhausted.

Fred's fellow jockeys spontaneously applauded him as he returned to the weighing room to sit, with lungs still aching, on the scales.

Dave Dick, who had survived two blunders by Pas Seul during the race, said after the race 'I've no doubt now that Fred is the best I ever saw, and there won't be another like him'.

The next day Fred went to Hurst Park and won the Grey Talk Hurdle on Firecracker, trained by Ken Cundell for Sir George Bailey, in a stern finish with Naratious Lad and Aberdonian. He rounded off the week by getting Cantab home a head winner in the Triumph Hurdle, holding off Anzio.

The following Monday, Fred received a letter from Lord Cottenham which expressed the gratitude of all those connected with Saffron Tartan. It said:

Dear Fred

Last October you said to us in a letter 'I hope I fulfil your trust in me'. You now know how well placed our trust was. We never wanted anyone else to ride Saffron, and in the words of Don Butchers, 'I don't honestly believe that anyone else could have got Saffron past the post first'.

I have never seen anyone ride such a copybook race. We and old Saffron must be so very grateful for the way you carried him along between the last two and lifted him over the last and up that hill to the post. The work of a great artist, for which we want to sincerely thank you.

Naturally we are so terribly pleased for the old horse's sake – a horse whom Vincent originally said was the best he had ever been privileged to train, and whom Don has since cared for and trained so brilliantly.

But we are so pleased for you too, and for the fact that Saffron has played his part in giving you this gloriously successful week, which you so richly deserve. We send you our most sincere thanks and congratulations. Yours sincerely,

Cottenham.

The rest of the season pales beside this week, but there was one important event before Fred ended the season in third place in the jockeys' championship, behind Stan Mellor and Tim Brookshaw. This was the arrival at Ryan Price's stable of Kilmore.

CHAPTER NINE

STILL STANDS ALONE

Kilmore had been bought for £3,000 by three show business friends, Mr Nat Cohen, Mr Ben Rosenfeld, and Mr Pinky Taylor. The horse had had a reasonably successful career in Ireland, where he had run 54 times and won on 11 occasions, but when he arrived at Ryan Price's stable as a potential Grand National winner he was 11 years old.

Kilmore had his first race in England in the Kim Muir Memorial Challenge Cup at the Cheltenham March meeting. Fred had just won the Champion Hurdle on Eborneezer, and he hastily grabbed his overcoat and race glasses from his valet, Dave Stalker, and hurried down to the paddock to see his probable Grand National mount for the first time.

He was not happy with the glimpse he got as Mr Gay Kindersley rode Kilmore out on to the course. In fact his first reaction at seeing the diminutive horse was 'My God, if that's a Grand National horse . . .' One thing that did strike him though, was Kilmore's walk. It had a light, cat-like quality, and behind the saddle, he gave the impression of having a coiled spring within him.

In this amateur riders' race, Kilmore never found top gear and he trailed round sluggishly to finish sixth to Nicolaus Silver, the horse who was to win that year's Grand National. Fred looked sadly at Ryan Price when he met him after Kilmore's race. 'Oh, Ryan, what have you done to me,' he said.

It was not until 10 days later that he found out a bit more about his Aintree mount.

Cheltenham and Liverpool were closer than usual that year and there was no time for Fred to ride Kilmore in a race. Instead he drove down to Lingfield Park on a Sunday morning to ride him in a schooling gallop.

In company with two other horses, they jumped five fences, and while Kilmore's jumping was no more than adequate, he at least showed Fred that he knew how to get out of trouble.

He met the last fence but one all wrong, and Fred left him alone. Kilmore took one more very quick stride unbidden and flew over the fence, thus demonstrating to Fred that he had the brains to put things right himself if necessary.

The following Saturday, Fred rode Kilmore out on to the Aintree course a great deal happier than when he had first set eyes on Kilmore.

The race brought out two Russian horses for the first time, Grifel and Reljef, and though they took no part in the final battle, it added colour and interest to a National field which included two previous winners in Merryman II and Mr What as well as Wyndburgh, who had twice been second, and Team Spirit, whose moment of glory at Aintree would not come until three more seasons had passed.

Had Fred known Kilmore better than he did from just one schooling gallop, then he believes he would have beaten this field of Aintree stars :

He ran a most marvellous race and never put a foot wrong, but I think I made much too much use of him. He was always going too free with me, and we were never out of the first half dozen. Coming on to the racecourse for the last time, I was still there with a terrific chance, but then Bobby Beasley on Nicolaus Silver and Derek Ancil on Merryman II began to go away from us and we just ran on to finish fifth, about 10 lengths behind the winner.

Kilmore had one more race that season, in France, but though he jumped the Grand Steeplechase de Paris course

96

Above: **Dead beat – both of them.** Ryan Price looks Beaver II over as Fred dismounts from the weary horse after winning the Grande Course des Haies de Quatre Ans. Fred's second hard race on an afternoon when he was feeling like death

Right: 'So this horse jumped right across me, and I had no option. . . .' Fred and Arthur Freeman analysing a race incident in the weighing room at Cheltenham

Above: In a class of their own. Francis Chichester and Fred Winter talking at the 1962 'Men of the Year' luncheon at the Savoy Hotel. *Below:* Fred in his new role. At the start of a new season he watches as the team do their first canters on Mandown Lambourn

brilliantly, the speed at which the French jumpers went was far too good for him.

Off the bit almost the whole way, he was in touch with the leaders just over half a mile out and was then swamped as the French horses turned on the pace again.

Even so, Fred started the 1961–62 season in the knowledge that he had a pretty safe conveyance to look forward to for the next running of the Grand National if all went well. He also started the season with retainers to two of the country's most powerful stables. Fulke Walwyn, for whom he had ridden a number of winners the previous season, had insisted that he should take a retainer for his stable.

It was with some reluctance that Fred did so, because he was also retained to ride Saffron Tartan in all his races, and when warning Fulke that both Ryan Price's stable and Saffron Tartan would have to come before the Saxon House runners, Fred felt sure that there would be many cases where there would be a clash of interests.

As it happened, Fred's first five rides for Fulke Walwyn produced four winners and a second and the arrangement with the Lambourn trainer worked out reasonably well throughout the season – more than reasonably, for he ended it by winning the Cheltenham Gold Cup and the Grand Steeplechase de Paris on Mandarin.

It was a season during which Fred was to ride his 800th winner, on Opening Bars at Fontwell Park on October 14. He also won three races at the big Cheltenham meeting, the French Four Year Old Champion Hurdle and the English Grand National as well as the Grand Steeplechase. But he tasted again the reverses that are capable of shattering the confidence of even the most hardened rider.

An early set-back was that Saffron Tartan broke down. He ran a fine race on his second appearance of the season, at Newbury in November, and was beaten five lengths when trying to give a stone to Frenchman's Cove, but soon after he developed leg trouble and it was decided there was little chance of such a heavy-topped horse being made right again. Saffron Tartan was retired from racing, but until he died late in 1968 he could still be seen enjoying himself on Newmarket Heath in the mornings, acting as a hack for young trainer Bill Watts.

On November 5, a racing journalist wrote 'Winter, though drawing inevitably towards the end of his riding days, still stands as he has done for so long – alone'.

The following day Fred started the longest losing run of his whole career. Between November 6 and November 17 he rode 32 horses, many of them well fancied, and every one was beaten. Finally, Some Alibi, trained by Fulke Walwyn, and Owen Davis from Ryan Price's stable, won for him at Sandown Park.

Fred breathed a sigh of relief, and on the way home in the car he went through the form book to weigh up the chances of his mounts on the second day of the meeting. They included his old friend Pouding in the three miles Walton Green Chase. Sandown was Pouding's favourite course, and he must surely have a reasonable chance now that the luck had turned.

But misfortune struck again. Pouding was up with the leaders when he fell a mile from home, and Fred needed no doctor to tell him that he had fractured his collar bone. He was out of the saddle until the next Sandown Park meeting, on December 6, when he came back with a winner, Clear Round, from Fulke Walwyn's stable.

While he was on the sidelines, Fred had to watch Mandarin win the Hennessy Gold Cup at Newbury with another rider on his back. This was that quiet, polished Irishman Willie Robinson whom Fulke Walwyn had seen riding in Ireland on a number of occasions. Mandarin was allowed to start at 7 to 1, and there was a big gamble on the Irish mare Olympia.

Pat Taaffe moved Olympia rapidly up from the rear of the field three-quarters of a mile from home, but two fences out Willie Robinson drove Mandarin up to head her, and the Hennessy horse ran on gamely to beat John O'Groats and Taxidermist for a popular win in the race sponsored by his owner's family firm.

Fred, watching at home on television, had mixed feelings about the win. He was delighted for the sake of Madame Hennessy and for the Walwyn stable, but he also knew that in this highly competitive game, it would be as well if he won on Mandarin next time he sat on the little horse. Otherwise, it might be Willie who would get the rides in future.

There is great camaraderie between National Hunt jockeys, but there is also great competition for the good rides. They daily risk their necks together and few would do anything deliberate which would endanger the life of another, but to stand and watch another jockey ride a horse which, but for injury, you would be on, brings out a peculiar mixture of feelings towards another human being whom you may admire a great deal. Maybe he could *just* lose by a length or so today.

Fred's worries concerning Mandarin were soon settled. Success came frequently, after he returned with a mended collar bone in mid-December, and he quickly settled into a winning streak for both Ryan Price and Fulke Walwyn, the peak of which was a glorious day at Kempton Park on January 25, when he rode four winners, including What a Myth and Mandarin, who defeated the Queen Mother's horse The Rip in a hard-fought Walter Hyde Handicap Chase.

Mandarin won by half a length. The Rip had won his last four races, was receiving eight pounds from Mandarin, and went on to win his next race. The form looked good and hopes of a Gold Cup win for Mandarin mounted.

Mandarin did not run again before Cheltenham, and for Fred the National Hunt meeting did not start auspiciously, for his three mounts on the first day were all unplaced. So too were his first two mounts on the Wednesday, but then

99

Ryan Price sent him out to win the three miles handicap hurdle on St Stephen, and on the final day his last mount of the meeting Sky Pink won the County Handicap Hurdle.

But before the bowler hats, the tweeds, the Jaguars, the Irish priests and the picnic baskets had left Cheltenham Fred had ridden one of his greatest races on Mandarin in the Gold Cup.

The Gold Cup started nearly half an hour later than intended for right up to the last moment frost had put racing in doubt and it was only at one o'clock that the Stewards took the decision in icy sunshine that racing would be possible if all the events were put back 25 minutes.

There was great confidence behind Fortria, who had won eight races the previous season, including the National Hunt Champion Chase over two miles at Cheltenham. Fortria had not won a race since then, except a walk-over in Ireland, but even in defeat he had shown that he stayed longer distances. He had also put up some great weight-carrying performances, such as when he only just failed to give 16 lb to Scottish Memories in the Mackeson Gold Cup at Cheltenham in November.

Pas Seul was in the field, too, but all was not well with the Gold Cup winner of two seasons back. With radar-like precision, the betting market assessed his chances of overcoming the opposition and whatever other forces were at work.

He had won four of his last five races and looked as good a horse as ever, but rumours were circulating about him before the race. For three days during the previous week Pas Seul had suffered from kidney trouble, but his trainer, Bob Turnell, was confident that he had recovered from this. There were plenty of people willing to back Pas Seul, but he went from 15 to 8 on in the ante-post betting to 9 to 4 against at the off – an almost unprecedented drift in a race such as this.

At the ditch opposite the stands, Pas Seul made a frightful blunder and by the water jump second time round, with a mile to go, Dave Dick was not at all hopeful about his chances. Somehow he drove Pas Seul up into the front line as they turned for home, but that was the end and Pas Seul weakened to finish a distant fifth.

When Mandarin jumped the water for the second time, Fred just did not believe that he could win:

He had been hunting round, going nicely within himself, but then they turned the tap on and in three strides Mandarin was off the bit and in trouble. Four or five horses went past me and I was driving Mandarin for all I was worth and not making any ground on the leaders. Just at the top of the hill, with about half a mile to go, I could see a gap right down the rails and I thought, if we're going to do any good, we've got to go up there.

I gave the old fellow a crack with the whip and he simply flew. He went up three places straight away until he got to Fortria. We jumped the last but one on his tail and when we got to the elbow Pat Taaffe was not clear enough to move over to the rails in front of us. As soon as we met the rising ground, I thought we might just win, but right up to that point Pat was going better than me. It was a hell of a fight up the hill, but we beat Fortria a length. It was purely Mandarin's courage that won the race.

There was a tumultuous reception for Fred and Mandarin as they returned to the winner's enclosure. It was Mandarin's third attempt at the race and by now the courageous heart which was hidden in so small a frame had made him one of the most popular horses to race for many years.

Fred went on to Hurst Park and won the Grey Talk Hurdle, for the third year running, this time on Barbizon, but he was soon reminded of the speed at which the racing public can change their views about a rider when he was defeated on Catapult II, the 7 to 4 favourite for the Triumph Hurdle the following day.

Ryan Price ran two horses in the race – Catapult II and Beaver II, ridden by Josh Gifford. Catapult came from France with a big reputation and had won a race there already, while Beaver II, who also came from across the Channel, had won two of his last three races, though not in particularly good company.

Though it was by now obvious that Beaver II was useful, he did not appear to be anything out of the ordinary, and he was allowed to start at 100 to 6 for the Triumph.

I must admit that I rode rather a bad race on Catapult. There was a very good looking horse of Lord Derby's in the field called Tudor Treasure, who was a very free runner and not a good jumper. I had seen him a couple of times and he didn't look very courageous to me, and my idea was to take him on with Catapult, as I was sure he would turn it in. Unfortunately, I did it much too soon. I went to the front well before we turned into the straight, and while Tudor Treasure got discouraged sure enough, my horse hadn't got much left in him when Josh Gifford came sailing along on this little Beaver II and went by to beat us six lengths, looking an absolute champion. The remarks from the crowd you can just imagine.

What the sportsmen who were making all the noise did not know, and neither did the Price stable, was that within a very short space of time, Beaver II was to prove himself a real champion showing that, however badly Fred may have felt that he rode Catapult II, his horse was taking on an impossible task in trying to give Beaver II seven pounds.

And so to Aintree.

Neither Ryan Price nor Fulke Walwyn had anything better in their stables for Fred to ride at Liverpool than Kilmore, who had run so well to finish fifth in the previous season's

Grand National, but there were moments during the months leading up to the big race when Fred had doubts about his mount.

Kilmore had started off well enough by running second to John O'Groats under a big weight at Folkestone. But then he returned to Aintree for the Becher Chase at the November meeting, and fell at the sixth fence. At the time, Fred could not really understand why the horse had done it. Later he was to discover that the fault was his own.

Next Kilmore ran in the Hennessy Gold Cup, ridden by Josh Gifford. The horse finished out of the first half dozen, but he was in the leading group for a long way, and his owners were not disappointed by his performance.

Another satisfactory outing followed in the Mildmay Memorial Chase at Sandown Park on January 13, when Kilmore finished fifth. Ryan Price then decided to give Kilmore a good rest and a pre-National tune-up in a race at Lingfield Park on March 21, ten days before the big event. For the second time this season, Kilmore finished on the floor :

I had got the idea that the only thing to do to make sure he stayed the distance at Liverpool was to settle him down and not make so much use of him as I had in the previous National. So at Lingfield, to put this into practice, I dropped him out early on. He settled well and was jumping absolutely super. Then going into the open ditch about a mile and a quarter out I started to ask him to put the speed on and get into the race with a chance.

I gave him a kick going into the jump and the next moment we were on the floor. It had been just the same when he fell in the Becher Chase, and really I think it was lucky that he fell at Lingfield. It opened my eyes and showed me that, once I had got him settled and popping over his fences happily, it was wrong to suddenly ask him to race faster and jump bigger. When I went to Liverpool I was determined that one thing I would never do was to make a move on him.

So in the National, Fred sat still and let Kilmore do it all himself. The race was run under appalling conditions, with heavy rain and recent frosts reducing the going to a horrible sort of porridge. This clearly suited neither the previous year's winner, Nicolaus Silver, nor Merryman II, who had won two years earlier and had then been second to Nicolaus Silver. It did not suit a lot of the other runners, too, but the slower pace was probably responsible for the record number of 17 out of the 32 runners completing the course.

The 7 to 1 favourite Frenchman's Cove was going well when he was brought down at the 19th fence, but his subsequent performances suggested that even if he had stayed on his feet, it is doubtful if he would have heart for an all out struggle on the long run from the last fence to the winning post in the rain and mud.

As they turned for home at the Canal the second time, Fred had Kilmore in about sixth place going well within himself, while the two Irish outsiders Gay Navaree and Fredith's Son disputed the lead, with Mr What, Nicolaus Silver and Wyndburgh, already runner-up in two Nationals, close behind.

It was not until they had jumped the last fence but one that Fred let Kilmore go to the front, to the intense relief of the three part owners. They were becoming more and more depressed as they watched the race at home on television, with Kilmore just off the screen most of the way.

Wyndburgh battled on gamely and so did Mr What, but Kilmore was always holding them, and the distances were ten lengths, the same, as the rain-soaked crowd cheered Fred to his second Grand National win. As the horses passed the post, we suddenly realised that the old Aintree adage 'too old at twelve' had been proved completely false. The first three to finish were all twelve years old.

So Fred's theory had been right, and his Aintree 'route' justified again. He had never left the inside on Kilmore, and was never in any semblance of trouble with other horses. He had left Kilmore completely alone and the horse had jumped brilliantly the whole way. He had waited and waited, and this takes a great deal of courage in a race like the Grand National. It was undoubtedly Fred's best ride ever at Aintree.

It was also a wonderful triumph for Ryan Price, who had already won nearly every big race in the Calendar, but never the National. Before the race he had said with the downright confidence that is so characteristic of him: 'Barring accidents, Kilmore will win.' The Captain really looked as though he meant it when he said in the unsaddling enclosure afterwards 'This is the greatest moment of my life.'

CHAPTER TEN

AND GENTLEMEN IN ENGLAND
NOW ABED

Soon after the Grand National, Fred announced that he was going to apply for a licence to ride on the flat for the first time since 1942, and for some reason this sparked off rumours that he was about to retire from steeplechasing. At Sandown Park's Royal Artillery meeting, he was both widely congratulated for his great win the previous Saturday on Kilmore, and kept busy answering pressmen who wanted to know if he was retiring at the end of the season.

The answer was an emphatic 'No', and he told the *Daily Sketch*'s John Rickman that he would be going on for at least a couple of seasons, if not more. And, as if it was needed, to show that there was life in the old dog yet, he won a hard fought selling hurdle on Rattler that day, and then made four journeys within the next week to four different racecourses – Wincanton, Folkestone, Taunton and Cheltenham – to ride four consecutive winners.

The application for a flat racing licence, which was quickly granted, had been inspired by a visit Fred had made to the Turkish baths the previous November. He noticed that, though he was not wasting particularly hard, he weighed only 9 st 7 lb stripped. It suddenly struck him that the maximum weights for flat racing had just gone up from 9 st 7 lb to 10 st, and that if he tried a little harder he could fit into that range and ride on the flat.

It could pay good dividends, and there seemed no reason why he should not continue to ride on the flat for another

10 years or so after he had decided to retire from the National Hunt scene.

Fred reckoned that he could lose another 10 lb easily, and with riding gear he would go to the scales at about 9 st 2 lb. He wrote to his father and asked him what he thought of the idea, and Fred Winter, senior, replied that if Fred could do that weight, he for one would be prepared to give him a chance. So in February, with about six weeks to go before the start of the flat racing season, Fred started to shed weight while he was still riding over jumps.

There were several offers of help when he announced his intention. Scobie Breasley's wife, May, rang up Diana and said that she had got a wonderful diet that Scobie used. She offered to send Fred the diet sheet. Fred started to try harder with his wasting than he had done for a long time, and the pounds began to roll off – to start with.

When he went out to ride Kilmore, set to carry 10 st 4 lb in the Grand National, Fred weighed only 9 st 4 lb without riding gear. The first few pounds had been easy, but then it became really tough going and he had to battle to lose every pound.

Fred also re-discovered the difference between flat race riding and National Hunt riding. He had about eight rides and the nearest he came to victory was to be beaten a neck and a short head into third place on Spaniard's Close, trained by his father, in a race at Brighton.

The fact is that while Fred and his colleagues such as Stan Mellor and Tim Brookshaw had special skills of their own, and enormous courage, those skills do not necessarily apply in flat racing.

No jumping jockey, except perhaps Bryan Marshall, has ever gone a shorter way home than Fred, but they might be the only riders in a race really concentrating on saving ground. In a flat race, *every* jockey on a fancied horse is trying to find the shortest way to the winning post. Everything happens, too, at greater speed than in jumping.

The biggest thrill for Fred during the flat season was to be engaged by Noel Murless to ride Lady Sassoon's good horse Sunny Way in the Northumberland Plate, with 10 stone, a weight which had never been carried in that race before. Unfortunately Sunny Way never got into the front line, and finished out of the first half dozen.

For Fred, the flat racing experiment was a complete flop and he quickly appreciated the particular talents of the top class flat jockeys, against whom he had not ridden for so many years.

'You can't teach an old dog new tricks,' was his summing up of the venture, but there was one blessing that came out of the experiment. This was that he had proved to himself that he could get down to riding weights around the 9 st 10 lb mark without too much trouble, even if weights below that were almost unattainable.

There was good reason in the early summer of 1962 for Fred to want to achieve such a weight. In the spring, both Ryan Price and Fulke Walwyn were laying plans for full-blooded attacks on the rich jumping prizes in France. It was to prove one of the most exciting forays against France since the Battle of Trafalgar, and Fred was to play a leading role.

Ryan Price's plan was to send Gold Wire, now owned by Mr Bob McCreery, and the Triumph Hurdle winner Beaver II, now owned by Mr Jack Sullivan, over to France to run in one or more races at Auteuil, the jumping course within a few minutes drive of the centre of Paris. Beaver's principal race was to be the Four Year Old Champion Hurdle.

For Mandarin, winner of the Cheltenham Gold Cup, the objective was a second tilt at the Grand Steeplechase de Paris, the so-called French Grand National over 4m. and 110 yards of the most devious course and jumps ever devised. In the 1960 race Mandarin had been a close second to Xanthor, finishing very fast after making a bad mistake.

As the English National Hunt season drew to a close, Fred, Diana and the children drove down to Cornwall for a holiday which was to be interrupted by four flying visits to France.

The Cornish air did not help Fred much in his efforts to keep his weight down. His appetite was sharpened and it was at about this stage that he realised what a difficult task he had set himself in trying to keep down to a reasonable flat racing weight.

On May 26, Fred set out from Cornwall on the long journey to Auteuil, where he was due to ride Beaver II in a preliminary race for the Four Years Old Champion Hurdle. Beaver II needed the outing badly, and he finished sixth.

His new owner, Mr Sullivan, was not particularly pleased with the performance, but in Fred's opinion Beaver II had run well and had jumped superbly. Beaver II now really had the feel of a horse who might one day win a Champion Hurdle at Cheltenham, whatever he might do in his coming race against the top French four-year-old hurdlers.

Fred flew back to England but returned again five days later to ride Gold Wire in a $2\frac{3}{4}$m. 'chase. He grumbled somewhat at being brought back from Cornwall to ride Gold Wire in what was really a preliminary outing over the continental type of fences before going for a more valuable event later in the month. To Fred's and Ryan Price's surprise, Gold Wire won a length from Dragon Vert, a horse who went on to win many good races. It was Fred's first win outside England.

Fred went back to Cornwall again, but before he rode Mandarin and Beaver II in their big races on June 17, he still had to make another flying visit to France to ride Mandarin in a school at Lamorlaye, the training village which is virtually part of the superbly appointed complex of gallops and tracks constituting Chantilly.

Mandarin had gone well when ridden by flat race jockey Jimmy Lindley in a gallop after racing at Newbury and had then been flown across from England several days before the big race. He did not seem to be worried by his new surroundings. He looked magnificent when Fred went to mount him in the yard of Chantilly trainer Alec Head where he was lodged.

It was a very hot morning, but Mandarin seemed to be in his element. He pulled as hard as he had ever done and went into his schooling gallop perhaps faster than Fred would have liked. But he jumped all the important fences brilliantly, including a great number of white rails and the bullfinch. The latter is not a test of jumping ability so much as courage, for the horses have to burst through a thin screen of hedge above the jump itself.

Mandarin revelled in his schooling session and Fred had the greatest difficulty in pulling him up to go back to the stables.

Fred flew back to England again with a week to go before the big day, and really began to worry about his weight, which had crept up to 10 st 3 lb. Two days before he was due to set off for France again, this time accompanied by Diana, he cut down his intake to almost nothing.

The day before the big race, Fred and Diana travelled up to London to stay at the Normandy Hotel, where they were joined by Diana's aunt, Mrs Doreen Beddington. Fred then made the mistake of sitting down to a very good dinner. It seemed all right at the time, for he now had the weight situation fairly well in hand and thought he could risk a good meal if he spent the night in the Turkish baths. Unhappily, his stomach, after two days' fasting, was in no condition for three White Ladies before a dinner which included avocado pear, Steak Diane and a couple of glasses of wine. Halfway through the meal, Fred knew it was a mistake, and by the end of it he felt very sick.

He left the hotel to spend the night in the Turkish baths with another pound to go before he was safely within the 9 st 10 lb that Beaver II had to carry. Walking through the streets, Fred felt far from well, but when he arrived at the Jermyn Street baths he went straight into the steam room.

Within five minutes he had to come out again for fresh air, and he then retired to the lavatory where he came out in a cold sweat and was extremely sick.

It was a limp and wretched Fred who accompanied Diana and Mrs Beddington to London Airport the next morning. He had been up all night being ill and he was hardly in the right condition for a man who was about to ride in the most competitive steeplechase of the French season.

At the airport, half the racing world seemed to be there and wanted to wish Fred good luck, and he tried to put on a cheerful face. On the plane he took the bold decision to have half a bottle of champagne. It would either put him right or finish him off. Fortunately it worked, though by the time he reached Auteuil he was still feeling considerably less fit to ride in an important race than ever before in his career.

The Grand Steeplechase was not due to start until after 4 p.m. Fred filled in some of the time by walking the course, part of which he had covered when he won a fortnight earlier on Gold Wire.

At last the jockeys were summoned to the paddock and the field paraded in front of an enormous crowd, which included more Englishmen than had ever before attended a French jumping meeting. As Fred cantered Mandarin to the starting gate, he was glad to be doing something at last.

The horse beneath him felt right. Mandarin was never an imposing animal, but he seemed to be thriving in the hot sunshine, he was carrying more weight than ever before, there was a lightness in his step. Fred felt distinctly better than he had a few hours earlier.

At 4.11 p.m. the starter sent the 14 runners on their journey of 4m. 110 yards. Just over $8\frac{1}{4}$ minutes later Fred Winter dismounted from Mandarin after experiencing one of the most frightening races of his life.

Mandarin, always a hard puller, was wearing a rubber-covered bit to protect his mouth. He settled down well enough and jumped the third fence up with the leaders. But

111

coming to the next jump, a six foot high privet fence, the metal of his bit snapped in his mouth under its rubber covering and Fred suddenly found himself without any contact – no way of steering Mandarin over the next 21 fences of the complex figure-of-eight course.

Fred was now in the appalling situation of sitting on a horse galloping at about 30 miles an hour and with no real means of control.

The first thought that went through my mind was 'sabotage', but after that I was too busy to think much more about that. Luckily the first four fences after it happened were in a straight line, so there was not much problem. The amazing thing was that Mandarin didn't try to run away. He was normally a free little devil, but he never attempted to go mad, and he never varied his speed one way or the other.

The next thing I thought was 'Well I'm not going to jump off'. I never have, because I was much too windy. Then I thought that when we got to the end of the straight row of fences and had to swing to the left, he would probably go straight on anyway, and I would have to jump off because there's an enormous wire barricade.

But by that time, I was beginning to find that I was able to move Mandarin about a fair bit with pressure from my knees. Also he was reacting to the feel of the reins on his neck. By the time that we came to the first bend, several of the French jockeys had realised the jam I was in. Daumas, who was on my outside on Taillefer, actually helped me round the first bend. He was about half a neck behind me and he swung Taillefer in so that the pressure of his horse and my own efforts got us round.

It was not until the field passed the stands again that Mandarin's many English supporters realised the dreadful predicament that Fred was in. One ring of the bit could be seen halfway up Mandarin's neck. There was a hum of amazement from the huge crowd as the field set out on the next tortuous circuit.

We came to this very tricky place with three courses to choose from. The one we had to take was in the middle. You have got about 50 yards of open space before the privet hedge which divides the thing up. Mandarin was almost in front and he went a little bit to the left, but I managed to straighten him up and he took the middle course.

After that he always had company and was never actually in front by himself. The other jockeys weren't actually helping me now, but they certainly didn't try to hamper me or to run me out, which would have been the easiest thing in the world to do.

Then Mandarin made an awful mistake at the water the second time – pitched right on his nose. In fact, it was a good thing because it left me about fifth and the others gave me a lead round the bend. The worst part of all was before four fences from home where we had to take a very sharp turn to the right and then take the middle course. It's very open on the right, and there was no horse on that side of me. Mandarin could so easily have taken the inside course. In fact, for a couple of strides he really looked as though he was going to. I had to throw absolutely everything to the left, and he came back on course.

With just over three furlongs to go, Mandarin broke down. Fred felt him falter in his stride, but whatever pain Mandarin may have been in, he kept going. He jumped the last fence in front and responding to Fred's driving he headed for the winning post.

Halfway up the long run in he was still in front, with Fred incredibly conjuring as much out of him as if he was riding a finish under normal conditions.

To the English supporters in the stand, it looked as though the impossible was about to happen. Fred and Mandarin had steered their way to victory against inconceivable odds.

Suddenly, with 200 yards to go, they realised it was not all over. The black Lumino, four years younger than Mandarin, was putting in a run which must surely carry him past Mme Hennessy's horse before the winning post.

Fred was doing everything he could to wring the last effort out of Mandarin, but Lumino was travelling so much faster at the winning post, and was in front two strides beyond, that no one in the stands could say who had won.

The moment he passed the post, Fred stopped riding, and Mandarin, exhausted and now really feeling his injured leg, immediately came down to a walk. Perhaps the judge knew before seeing the photograph, but neither Fred, nor Lumino's jockey, Kirchhofer, could say who had won this incredible race.

A photograph taken as the tired jockey and horse walked back towards the unsaddling enclosure, shows a despondent and tired Fred slumped on Mandarin's back. There is another taken two strides later when the loudspeaker had announced that Mandarin was the winner. Fred's transformed face and the broad smiles of Mme Hennessy, of travelling head lad Darkie Leatham and Mandarin's lad, 'Mush' Foster, walking beside the horse recreate the elation of all Mandarin's supporters at this moment.

It was not only the English contingent who had appreciated the true drama of the situation. Thousands in the crowd had seen what was happening as Mandarin fought his way to the front with his bridle flapping loosely round his neck.

There were those in the crowd, hardened racing men who had seen many a drama and many a brave horse, who admitted afterwards that they could scarcely see the finish for tears.

As Mandarin, covered in sweat and with his head down, completely exhausted, was greeted by his now jubilant trainer and hundreds of his English supporters, the cheering reached a crescendo.

114

The jubilation in the unsaddling enclosure was enormous. Fred slipped down from the saddle, undid the girth, patted Mandarin on his damp neck, and stumbled through a maze of congratulations to the weighing room door. He never knew how he made it. While everything had been happening in the race and he had had something to think about the whole time, it was different, but now his stomach pains returned.

Fred climbed on to the scales, then staggered back towards the stairs leading to the jockeys' room. All the French riders wanted to add their congratulations and shake his hand. They crowded round him. Fred was rocking on his feet, and it was Stan Mellor, due to ride Beaudeer against little Beaver II in the Champion Four Years Old Hurdle, who came to his rescue. 'I have never seen a man in such depths,' said Stan later. You would think he would be too weak to ride again for days, let alone go out half an hour later.'

Stan literally had to dress Fred like a baby, put his whip in his hand, accompany him to the scales and shepherd him out to the paddock past hundreds who still wanted to congratulate him.

Fred managed a bleak smile, couldn't remember afterwards what he said to Ryan Price and Beaver's owner in the paddock, and went out to ride a perfectly judged, hard fought race to win the hurdle by a length.

Fred kept the Findon horse perfectly placed the whole way and challenged the leaders at the last hurdle to defeat the well fancied Chamant d'Or and Ouf by one length and three-quarters. Stan Mellor never held any hopes of repeating the Stratford form and Beaudeer trailed in last of the ten runners.

Fred returned to another great reception. For him one of the most telling moments was when he returned to the jockeys' room again after winning two of the most valuable French jumping races of the year — a total of £29,000 in first prize money, and a hefty chunk out of the potential earnings of the French jumping riders.

There was a time, particularly in French flat racing, when visiting jockeys were given a tough time, and there have been some nasty incidents in the past. It has changed recently as the international exchange of runners has increased and become commonplace, but the reaction of the French jumping jockeys first to Fred's predicament on Mandarin and then to his great victories was exceptional.

They had every opportunity to get rid of him as Mandarin wended his way round the tortuous course, but no one raised a finger against him. They flocked to congratulate him after Mandarin had won, and again after Beaver's success.

There is a comradeship amongst jumping jockeys in England which is unmatched in the more businesslike atmosphere of flat racing, and the brotherhood of those who risk their lives over jumps for our entertainment and their own comparatively meagre reward extends beyond any one country.

A huge headline said in one of the French papers the next morning

'THIS ASTONISHING VICTORY FOR FRIENDSHIP'.

Fred went back to his hotel in Paris to rest after racing, and he was fit enough later in the evening to join in the celebration party given by Mme Hennessy for all those connected with Mandarin, as well as many of those who had come from England to see a memorable race.

In at least one Paris club that night, the surprised locals heard an Englishman stand on a chair to declaim with remarkable clarity, considering the late hour, chunks of King Harry's speech before Agincourt: '. . . And gentlemen in England, now a-bed shall think themselves accurs'd they were not here and hold their manhoods cheap whiles any speaks that fought with us upon St Crispin's Day.' The speaker was about 400 years out with his date, but who the hell cared.

116

CHAPTER ELEVEN

I DIDN'T WANT IT TO FINISH

Fred stayed on in France to ride Gold Wire at Auteuil five days after that busy Sunday, but Gold Wire found the opposition stiffer than when he had run there earlier in the month and he did not manage to get into a place behind Lumino, the horse who had so nearly defeated Mandarin.

Fred and Diana flew back to London, and when they reached home they were staggered by the pile of congratulatory letters and telegrams which had accumulated.

It was really this that put Mandarin's win in perspective for them. The French papers had been lavish in their praise and had devoted huge spaces to pictures of Mandarin and his broken bridle, but it was not until they returned home that they began to fully appreciate what an impact the win had had on the English public and people in racing.

Particularly treasured is a letter from Clarence House, signed by Sir Martin Gilliat, Private Secretary to Queen Elizabeth the Queen Mother:

Dear Fred,

Queen Elizabeth the Queen Mother has asked me to send you her warmest congratulations on your wonderful victory on Mandarin yesterday. Her Majesty arrived back from Canada at midday and the news of your success was a wonderful tonic on her return home.

It must have been quite a race and I should think you were mighty relieved when you had him safely over the last fence, although the run-in must have seemed rather long.

Altogether it has brought tremendous happiness to a great many people, and I hope will be an encouragement to others to 'have a go' in France – certainly Mandarin, Beaver and Vienna have kept the flag flying this year.

Perhaps we will get one of the Queen Mother's which will be worth taking over.

Again – many congratulations on a wonderful achievement.

Yours sincerely,

Martin Gilliat

The international adventures of Fred for this year had by no means finished, for a few weeks after he had returned from France, he was invited to Ireland to ride Carraroe in the Galway Plate. This 2m. 5f. handicap 'chase is the richest race at the traditional August meeting at Galway, and it gave Fred his first ride in Ireland.

Carraroe was a ten-year-old mare who had won her last two races, and Fred had good reason to remember her, for she had won the race at Sandown Park two seasons earlier when Saffron Tartan had shattered everyone by falling just before he was due to run in the Gold Cup. Carraroe was then trained by Cyril Mitchell at Epsom, but she was now back in Ireland, where she was bred, with 'Phonsie' O'Brien, brother of Vincent O'Brien.

Her owner, Mrs Miles Valentine, who maintains a stable of hunters in Pennsylvania, and has a string of racehorses in the States, flew from New York to Shannon Airport and then drove to the racecourse to see her mare run, arriving only half an hour before the race. It was well worth the effort, for Fred rode a superb race to win by half a length. The crowd welcomed him like a hero, but when you look at it his performance was just such as he had given on many previous occasions – a combination of determination, patience, and jockeyship.

Carraroe made a bad blunder seven fences from home and

118

lost several lengths. Fred gave her plenty of time to recover, and coming to the second fence from home he knew he had a good chance of winning.

Carraroe then frightened the life out of him by almost neglecting to jump. 'I really thought we had had it,' he said afterwards, but somehow Carraroe survived and in a flash Fred got the mare going to take the last fence, only 50 yards away, within half a length of the leaders, Dandy Hall and Height O' Fashion. It was Height O' Fashion whom she narrowly beat into second place.

The crowd shouted 'Come back again, Fred' after watching him dismount in the unsaddling enclosure. He did make one more visit to Ireland – to Powerstown Park just over a year later – and rode another winner, San Marco.

Yet another country, America, was to see Fred in action for the first time before 1962 was out.

In the autumn, ex-jockey Aubrey Brabazon, who won two Champion Hurdles and three Cheltenham Gold Cups, on Hatton's Grace and Cottage Rake between 1948 and 1951, and was now training in Ireland, asked Fred if he would go to Belmont Park to ride Moonsun for Mr Jack Sullivan. The objective was the Temple Gwathmey Chase, the most valuable event in the American jumping calendar.

The necessary business of riding at little meetings was still going on. Fred had had his first rides of the 1962–63 season at Devon and Exeter and his first win on Greenhills Lad in a selling hurdle there. His visit to America was sandwiched between two successful rides on Mr Bernard Myers' hurdler Little Smokey, in £170 races at Huntingdon and Wincanton – somewhat less glamorous courses than tree-lined Belmont Park on Long Island, five miles from Idlewild Airport into which Fred and Diana flew two days before Moonsun was due to run.

Moonsun had himself been flown out several days earlier and was settled in the stables at Belmont Park. He was a useful five-year-old, who in his most recent race had run second at Listowel to Height O' Fashion, the horse that Fred had beaten on Carraroe. The going that day had been as deep as it can be in Ireland. At Belmont the jumping track was like concrete.

Fred and Diana stayed with Mrs Betty Fraser Horn, who later married our knowledgeable and experienced stipendary steward, Brigadier 'Roscoe' Harvey. She introduced them to many people in American steeplechasing and they were flattered by American hospitality at its best.

On the night they arrived they went out to dine with Moonsun's owner, Mr Jack Sullivan, at his Long Island home and there they met Pete Bostwick. He and his brother Mike had ridden as amateurs in England between the wars and won many races. Pete had become one of America's leading jumping trainers and he asked Fred if he would ride one of his runners, Baby Prince, over hurdles at Belmont Park the next day.

It was fortunate for Fred that he did, for otherwise the trip would have been abortive. The next morning he jogged out on to the exercise track on Moonsun, wearing a regulation American crash helmet, and schooled the Irish horse over three fences.

When he walked Moonsun back to where Aubrey Brabazon, Diana and Jack Sullivan were standing, he could only report that the ground was far too hard for him. The only decision could be not to run him in the big race, for the outcome would probably have been a badly broken down horse.

However, in the afternoon, the disappointment of not having a ride in the Temple Gwathmey was eased when Fred won the New York Turf Writers' Cup on Baby Prince.

This four-year-old, who looked more like a flat racehorse than a jumper, already held the track record for $2\frac{1}{4}$ miles over the thin brush hurdles at Belmont Park. Jumping is not always the word to describe this game, for some of the horses barely left the ground.

120

Fred soon had Baby Prince settled in fourth place. He found the bends on the mile and a quarter course, tucked inside the flat track, beautifully cambered, and he was always happy with the way his horse was going on ground which was officially described as 'hard'.

He let Baby Prince go to the front after the eleventh hurdle and after that he never saw another horse, winning by three and three-quarters of a length from English exile Tommy Walsh on Shantyboat. Without much effort, Baby Prince had skittled round in seven seconds less than his own record.

The American turf writers knew all about Fred's recent exploits on Mandarin and paid ample tribute to him in their columns the next day. There was reward, too, for stable jockey Tommy Walsh, who had given up the ride on Baby Prince, for he won the Temple Gwathmey the following afternoon on Pete Bostwick's horse Barnaby's Bluff. Ironically for the connections of Moonsun, snow had now fallen and by the time the big race was run, the going was soft.

It is sad to think that American jumping on metropolitan courses is literally struggling for its life. At a time when English steeplechasing has never been more popular, the city-born American racegoer has little time for the jumping events which are somewhat reluctantly included in racing programmes by managements who can point to the fact that the fans' dislike of seeing their money 'in the air' is directly reflected in lower tote turnover. Only Aqueduct, Belmont Park, Saratoga, Monmouth Park and Delaware Park now stage jumping races. It is perhaps among the enthusiasts of hunt racing, amateur though they may be, that the real spirit of American jumping is to be found. It was from this quarter that Jay Trump was to emerge later to play such an important part in Fred's story.

Fred returned to England to win again on Little Smokey at Wincanton, now having ridden winners in four countries during the year. He was widely congratulated everywhere he went, and even though he was going through a period when his average of winners was well below his usual figure of over 20 per cent – his 72 rides from November to December 22 produced only eight winners – he was always in the news.

On November 15, he was one of the guests of honour at the 'Men of the Year' luncheon at the Savoy Hotel, London. There he met Francis Chichester, who had still to bring off his greatest feat in sailing round the world single-handed, but at this time was being honoured for his lone transatlantic crossing in record time. 'A strange, quiet man who didn't look very happy with his surroundings' was how Fred recalled the great sailor.

Three days later Fred was honoured at the traditional dinner given at the Queen's Hotel, Cheltenham, by the Cheltenham Steeplechase Company, for the champion National Hunt jockey. Holder of the title was, of course, not Fred but Stan Mellor, though four times in the past it was Fred who had occupied the place of honour at the top table and replied to the toast made by the current Senior Steward.

This was Stan's dinner, but everyone present was delighted when Lord Willoughby de Broke announced that the organisers of the dinner had decided that they could not allow this annual gathering of jumping professionals, amateurs and enthusiasts to go by without marking the magnificent exploits of Fred Winter in four different countries during the past year.

The trophy which Lord Willoughby handed to Fred amongst huge applause was a pair of china bonite galloping horses. These had just been imported from Peking and were thought to be extremely suitable for presentation to the man whose name was so closely linked with Mandarin.

The round of dinners to which Fred was invited was still not complete. Early in January, Fred was back at the Savoy to represent racing at the Variety Club's luncheon. But by this time racing had come to a halt and Fred, like everyone else making a living from the sport, faced a bleak and depressing time.

Frost prevented all of the nine meetings scheduled for Boxing Day from taking place. Then came the snow. Somehow Ayr missed the bad weather and racing took place there on January 5, but that was the end until Newbury on March 8. It was the worst winter in the history of National Hunt racing, and it brought serious financial problems to many people.

For Fred, who had been in the forefront of National Hunt jockeys for the past 15 years and had been earning at a much higher level than most, it was not too serious, though his outgoings would also be at a higher level than those of many of his colleagues.

But for a lesser jumping jockey with perhaps two children, a mortgaged house, and payments on the car to keep up, this was indeed a bleak winter, and so it was for racecourse staff and gatemen, for jockeys' valets, for horse box drivers and many others.

It was bad, too, for the racing journalist who had to find something to fill his column every day, but he at least had an assured income and a warm office from which to do his telephoning. In the training stables, morale sunk low as day after day, lads with freezing fingers and feet trotted horses on straw beds in the nearest accessible paddock.

At some training quarters they found it possible to keep the snow on one or two stretches of gallops harrowed and soft so that horses, with their hooves greased to prevent 'balling', could work for a while, but the arctic winds and frosts soon returned to end that by putting an impenetrable crust on the snow.

For the first month of the wintry spell, Fred quite enjoyed the rest from the routine of racing and driving to meetings.

After that it was boring, and very expensive. We did some skiing on the hills near home and toboganning with the

*children when they were back from school. I chopped a
tremendous amount of logs to keep the house warm. We had
an old hunter of my father's there, and I laid a straw ring in
the paddock next to the house. I used to trot and hack
canter him round that, so that by the time the thaw came,
and racing resumed, I was reasonably fit.*

Even so, Fred had to wait a while for his first winner. His
last ride before the bad weather came had been a winner,
Lord Weir's Ashburn at Fontwell Park on December 22.
This horse was also his first ride at Newbury on March 8,
but it was not until 10 days and 24 rides later that he won
on Mr Gerry Judd's Scottish Final at Worcester.

Unfortunately this period included the big meeting at
Cheltenham, which had been the scene of so many triumphs
for Fred in the past. Fred had a frustrating meeting, and
the nearest he could get to winning was to finish third on
the Irish mare Ivy Green in the Cathcart Challenge Cup
and third on Duke of York in the Gold Cup behind Willie
Robinson, who was on a new star in the steeplechasing
world, Mill House.

Kilmore, whom Ryan Price had been bringing along
gently in preparation for another tilt at the Grand National,
had his third outing of the season in the National Hunt
Handicap Chase. He jumped well enough and made up
some ground towards the end of the race, though he finished
a good many lengths behind the winner, the game little Team
Spirit, who had joined Fulke Walwyn's stable earlier in the
season from Ireland.

Kilmore, like almost everything else in the field, needed
the race after the long hold-up, and he went to Aintree on
March 30 much straighter in condition than he had been at
Cheltenham.

Fred started Grand National day well by winning both
divisions of the Liverpool Hurdle on horses trained by Ryan
Price – Pavot and Brocade Slipper. It was a great day for

Ryan because he also won one of the flat events with Valor II, ridden by Fred's brother-in-law Doug Smith, but the good luck did not extend to Kilmore in the big race.

Fred rode almost the identical race to that which had brought him victory twelve months earlier. He settled Kilmore down and 'hunted' round on him, leaving the little horse to work it all out for himself. What wrecked the plan was the fall of Mr Jones at the water jump. Mr Jones badly hampered Kilmore and in doing so, gave him a kick which slightly lamed him.

Fred could feel that there was something wrong with Kilmore as they set out on the second circuit, but Kilmore galloped on doggedly and Fred decided against pulling him up. Jumping perfectly, measuring each of the towering fences with precision, Kilmore slowly began to make up ground on the leaders again, but as they swung round the Canal Turn and headed for home, he had nearly 20 horses in front of him.

Kilmore began to pick off his rivals one by one, but halfway between the last two fences Fred realised that the task was almost impossible. John Lawrence on Carrickbeg was heading for home with high hopes of victory, which were to be dashed in the last agonising strides as Pat Buckley drove the 66 to 1 chance Ayala into a three-quarters of a length lead.

One of the loose horses interfered with Kilmore in the run-in, but there was by now no chance of him catching the leaders, and he galloped on at the same pace to finish sixth, about 22 lengths behind Ayala. It was a gallant performance in view of the trouble Kilmore had been in at the water.

After the drama of Liverpool, it was back to the bread and butter meetings. Fred's average began to improve, and in the period from April 9 to April 15, he rode eight winners. This record included four winners from his four only mounts at Newton Abbot. But lurking round the corner was more misfortune. Just as things were going better than they had done for a long time, the mat was whipped smartly from under Fred's feet.

The day after his four wins in Devonshire, he drove to Chepstow for several mounts, including Andy Capp in the first race, a two miles 'chase.

Andy Capp was backed down to start favourite at 9 to 4. Fred drove him into the last fence as he tried to get on terms with the leader, Perfect Poise, and Andy Capp hit the fence hard and fell heavily. It was some slight compensation that the ground was soft, otherwise Fred's injuries might have been more serious than they were.

He was examined on the course, but was allowed to go home. John Lehane drove him back to Stow-on-the-Wold and Fred went to bed feeling sharp pains in his chest. By the next morning he was in agony and decided to go up to London to see orthopaedic surgeon Bill Tucker, who X-rayed him. Three ribs were cracked.

Supporting bandages were put round Fred's chest and he went home to Gloucestershire feeling slightly better. So much so that when he reached Kitsbury, he decided to put on a sweat suit and mow the lawn as he thought it would not be long before he would be riding again. The weight would have to be watched while he was out of action.

It was Diana's birthday and a few friends came in for dinner. Fred had a couple of drinks before the meal and there was wine with the dinner. Suddenly, halfway through the main course he felt very ill. A giant hand seemed to be gripping his chest and preventing him from breathing. He left the party and went upstairs to lie down while Diana phoned for the local doctor.

He diagnosed fluid on the chest. The next day Diana drove Fred up to London again for further X-rays. It was an agonising journey. The doctor's findings were confirmed and Fred was sent straight to the London Clinic. That evening they operated on him for a punctured lung and drained away $5\frac{1}{2}$ pints of fluid. The infection took nearly a fortnight to clear up, and Fred's recovery from that Chepstow fall was slow and painful.

Fred did not ride again that season and his total of 29 wins was his lowest since the 1949–50 season (only his third as a National Hunt rider) when he rode 18 winners. Two things contributed to the small total. First and foremost the appalling winter and nearly three months without racing, and secondly his injury. But there was another factor.

I began to realise that I was not enjoying it at all that season. I did not enjoy it because I realised that on occasions I was being beaten when I should not have been beaten. I was blowing up a hundred yards before the winning post. I had always said to myself that when I came to the conclusion that I was not riding as well as I could, it would be a sign that my nerve had gone. You can't give value for money then. The only thing I really enjoyed in racing was winning. Being second or third was of no interest at all, and I decided that I was not winning often enough. The period between the start and the finish was not as much fun as it used to be. It was time to turn it in.

Fred had been thinking along these lines before his crashing fall at Chepstow. Those who saw him drive Andy Capp into the last fence might have had their own views about whether or not they were watching a man whose nerve was going, but at any rate Fred had already decided that he would start making a few enquiries that very week about jobs in racing that might keep him in touch with his weighing room colleagues when he retired.

On the day after his fall when he went up to London for an X-ray, he also called in at Weatherbys' offices in Cavendish Square to enquire about the possibilities of a post as a National Hunt starter. He was told that there was no chance of becoming a starter but it might be possible for him to be a judge.

The aloofness of that position and its remoteness from the jockeys and the horses during a race did not appeal to Fred. He was, in fact, extremely annoyed that Weatherbys' could not find a starters' job for a man whose experience and knowledge must have made him ideally suited for the post.

Fred left Cavendish Square in a bad frame of mind, to which his aching chest was contributing a good deal, and it was really at this moment that he decided that, if racing could not offer him the job that he wanted, he would have to become a trainer when he retired.

While he was recovering from his injury in the London Clinic, a personal and confidential letter arrived from Admiralty House, Whitehall, announcing that the Prime Minister was considering submitting Fred's name to the Queen with a recommendation that he should be appointed a Commander of the British Empire. Fred was amazed and delighted. He accepted for he felt it was a wonderful honour not only for himself but the whole of his profession. When the Birthday Honours List was published the following month the whole racing world was thrilled to hear of the C.B.E. that was to be conferred upon him.

A further honour was to come soon after he left hospital, for an invitation to luncheon at Buckingham Palace with the Queen and Prince Philip arrived.

They were a mixed bag who sat down to lunch at the Palace on June 11, 1963, including a dean, a headmistress, and a Minister of State, but there was also a skilful blending of those with interests not entirely remote from racing : Mr Edmund de Rothschild; Mr Peter Wilson, the chairman of Sotheby's and a man who has handled many paintings of well known racehorses; and Mr Wilson Stephens, the editor of *The Field*. Prince Philip, like Fred, had been in the wars recently. He had had a fall while playing polo and had badly bruised a shoulder.

Fred's orders from the doctors were that he was not to

'The day before the race, we crystallised the plan. He followed the route exactly and everything I told him'. Fred paces the Grand National course with Tommy Smith and owner Mrs Mary Stephenson before Tommy won the 1965 Grand National on Jay Trump

Jay Trump clears the last just ahead of Freddie. He won by six lengths. Fred watched from the stands: 'It was agony, sheer agony'

Tim Norman rides Anglo back to the unsaddling enclosure –
Fred's second Grand National winner in two seasons as a trainer

ride for two months after his Chepstow fall. He recuperated slowly during the summer of 1963, and while this might have appeared to be an ideal moment to announce his retirement, two things influenced him to go on riding during the coming season.

One of these was the impossibility of finding training quarters, staff, equipment, and horses in time to start training before the new season opened at Newton Abbot in August. The other was the news that his gallant Aintree partner Kilmore had recovered well from his Aintree injury and was now showing every evidence of being as spritely as ever, even though he would be 14 years old the following January 1.

With three superb rides on Kilmore at Liverpool behind him, Fred could think of nothing better to look forward to in his final season than a last ride round the Aintree course on Kilmore. He begged the owners to leave the horse in training and run him in the 1964 National.

On November 15, a few days after Mrs Ryan Price's Charlie Worcester had become his 900th winner, at Folkestone, Fred went into the press room at Cheltenham and broke the news that he had decided to retire at the end of the season.

He also told the press that his last day's riding would be at Cheltenham on Saturday, April 11, and that he intended to set up as a trainer and was looking for stables in the Lambourn area.

The news of his retirement occupied a great deal of space in papers both at home and abroad, particularly in France where his feat on Mandarin had made him the most popular English jockey ever to ride in that country, but it was not received with any surprise.

By now, Fred was 37 years old, and that is quite an age in a game as tough as National Hunt racing. He had been riding for 17 hard seasons, had fractured his spine, his skull, a leg, lost the top of a finger and broken a good many other bones. His latest chest injury had been one of the most unpleasant and painful of his career.

Yet racegoers were still to see the dogged Winter determination and courage time and again during this last season. The determination never more so than when he won an incredible race at Leicester in November during which each of the four runners was on the floor, including Fred's mount Carry On.

The trouble started when David Nicholson's horse Norwegian fell at the first fence. Then at the fifth, an open ditch, two more went. Clive Chapman's mount Kilvemnon fell and brought down King Fin, ridden by Phil Harvey. This left Fred alone on Carry On, and he knew immediately that the six-year-old would not like being on his own. However, King Fin, Norwegian and Kilvemnon, relieved of their riders, raced past Carry On and gave him a lead up the straight past the winning post for the first time.

But Fred guessed that it was highly likely that this experienced bunch of steeplechasers would know exactly where the racecourse's stables were and where their horseboxes were parked, and sure enough, as they made the turn away from the stands, they headed away from the rails and towards the gate leading to the stables.

Carry On was so busy turning his head to see where his carefree galloping companions were off to that he completely failed to see the water jump, the first jump in the back straight, and fell straight into it.

Fred was quickly on his feet and he caught his soaking wet mount as he scrambled out of the water. He jumped up and levered himself into the saddle, and amidst great cheering from the grand stands, set Carry On in the direction of the next fence, an open ditch. This was too much for Carry On, who firmly applied the brakes as he approached the fence and came to a dead stand.

Fred turned him and trotted back 20 yards, gave Carry

On a pat on the neck and a few words of encouragement, and set sail for the fence again.

This time Carry On slithered up to the guard rail, hit it and did a spectacular somersault into the ditch. Fred decided that the chances of getting him to negotiate this fence solo, let alone the eight others beyond it, were hopeless. He started to lead Carry On back towards the stands.

But other dramas were also being enacted. David Nicholson had run towards the racecourse stables, caught Norwegian and remounted him. He returned to the point at which they had departed from the race and set off again. It was a shortlived effort. Norwegian had decided that he had done enough for today, and after he had clambered over two fences with a great reluctance, David Nicholson pulled him up.

Meanwhile Kilvemnon's trainer, Maurice Bailey, had caught his mare and was riding her down the course in search of Clive Chapman, and Phil Harvey had been reunited with King Fin. These two returned to their point of departure and set off again, with the race apparently between them.

It was at this point that Ryan Price had a brilliant idea. Racing from the grand stand across the course he met a mud-plastered Fred leading Carry On back.

'What the hell do you want me to do now?' said Fred.

'Wait for the others coming round,' said Ryan, 'and if they get this far drop in behind them. Let them give you a lead.'

'It's no good,' said Fred. 'He won't jump that bloody ditch.'

'Yes he will. Tuck him in behind them, shut your eyes, and keep driving him. He'll jump it.'

He gave Fred a leg up. Carry On pricked his ears as he saw the other two horses coming towards him. Fred wheeled him in behind them and kicked him into a gallop. Sure enough, with the others to keep him company again, Carry On sailed over the open ditch. Fred kept him in behind the others until between the last two fences, when he drove him into the lead, and Carry On beat King Fin by three-quarters of a length to great cheering – particularly from those who had laid odds on him earlier when he was the only horse standing.

The prize that Carry On landed after all this effort was £173, and the time it took to achieve it was nearly thirteen minutes, almost double the average time for a three miles 'chase at Leicester.

The Queen Mother mentioned the incident the next day when Fred went to Buckingham Palace to receive his C.B.E. She was holding the investiture on behalf of the Queen, who was on a Royal Tour of Australia. 'It sounded very amusing,' she said as she placed the ribbon over Fred's shoulders, 'but was it as funny for you?'

'Well Ma'am, it wasn't at the time,' said Fred, 'but it was afterwards.'

A few days later, the Queen Mother herself had reason to recognise that there was not all that much wrong with Fred's riding in his final season.

Double Star, one of her favourites, was well fancied to win on a day when his stable companions Laffy and Makaldar were both successful at Lingfield Park. Always a difficult horse to beat on this course, Double Star was in the lead at the last fence, but Fred, only third at this point on Double March, rode a superb finish and beat the Queen Mother's horse a length.

A week later at Sandown Park, Fred became involved in an objection after he had beaten another of the Queen Mother's horses, Sunbridge. Riding What a Myth, who had just won his first two steeplechases with Fred in the saddle, he was first by half a length. At the last fence Sunbridge and What a Myth had collided, and to most people watching from the stands, it seemed that it was What a Myth who had veered towards the Queen Mother's horse and knocked him out of his stride.

But Fred knew that it was Sunbridge who had caused the trouble, and he became even more confident of the outcome of the objection that the Stewards themselves lodged against his horse when Sunbridge's rider, Willie Robinson, apologised to him for the collision as they rode back to the unsaddling enclosure.

It was one of the occasions when the head-on camera patrol shot showed exactly what had happened. The Queen Mother's horse had veered about 10 yards off a true line before hitting Fred's mount, rolled away, and then returned for another bump.

The Stewards withdrew their objection to What a Myth who, after Fred's retirement, was to win many good races for Ryan Price's stable.

Fred had been at his brilliant best in getting What a Myth home by half a length under difficult conditions and there must have been many who wondered that day why on earth he was retiring. And again when he rode five winners from six mounts at Sandown Park on January 29 and Windsor on February 1, while those who were at Newbury on February 29 can count themselves fortunate to be present at a vintage Winter performance – five rides and four winners, all achieved in different manner.

On Sally's Pal in the first race, a nicely timed run to take the lead two hurdles from home and a hard drive home on the flat to make sure that no one got to him.

On Vultrix in the $2\frac{1}{2}$ miles 'chase, up with the leaders all the way on a horse who could not be expected to find much finishing speed, Fred was driving, driving well before they turned into the long straight. He appeared to have no chance of catching the leader D'You Mind between the last two fences, but he won by half a length.

On Ballypru in the four-year-old hurdle, he led from start to finish and judged the pace impeccably; and then in the

133

maiden hurdle he brought Ringside to the front at the last hurdle and had to ride like a demon to win by a head.

It was a day full of nostalgia, for as the season ran out there were continual reminders that we were seeing something that we might never see again : a perfectionist in the art of riding over jumps. Fred might not be totally infallible, and he was always the first to admit it when he made a mistake. But for other jockeys probably the most depressing thing in the world, even at this late stage of his career, was the sight of Fred drawing up alongside them between the last two hurdles with his head down, whip up and his heels rhythmically driving his mount on the shortest route to the winning line.

Emphasising the mood at Newbury that day was the presence of the great Mandarin himself. His owner Mme Peggy Hennessy and trainer Fulke Walwyn had agreed that the little horse, who had been retired after his Grand Steeplechase de Paris win, should be brought over from Lambourn that day for the first running of the Mandarin Handicap Chase.

Wearing a rug in the Hennessy colours of gold and brown, presented to him by the Newbury Racecourse Company, Mandarin paraded down the course the length of the four enclosures. Hundreds flocked to the rails for a close-up of one of the bravest horses ever to race, while B.B.C. commentator Peter Bromley related over the loudspeakers the highlights of Mandarin's career. Fred's voice was also heard telling the story of that incredible win in France with the broken bridle.

It would be pleasant to record that Fred won the first running of Mandarin's race, but his mount, Red Thorn, finished only fourth behind Out and About. It was the only race open to professionals that day that Fred did not win.

April 11 at Cheltenham was still the deadline for Fred's

career, but it is just possible that, if Kilmore had won the Grand National again on March 21, he would have retired then. The old horse was giving him every encouragement to think that he had, at least, a fighting chance at Aintree. He had had only three races this season and had won the first two.

At Windsor in November, Kilmore had defeated a field all of whom were from five to seven years his junior, and he had then cantered round to beat some moderate opponents at Fontwell Park just after Christmas.

On his third appearance, it was no disgrace for him to be beaten six lengths by Pas Seul at Kempton Park in the Walter Hyde Handicap Chase. The Cheltenham Gold Cup winner of four seasons earlier still had a fair turn of foot, and a sharp course such as Kempton Park suited him much better than it did a one-paced stayer like Kilmore.

But before Kilmore ran in the Grand National, tragedy struck Ryan Price's stable. Rosyth, winner of the previous season's Schweppes Gold Trophy at Liverpool, returned to his best form in this £7,639 race when it was staged again, this time at Newbury, after running unplaced in all but one of his five races since his win. He immediately became the subject of a stewards' enquiry. Ryan Price was reported to the Stewards of the National Hunt Committee, who withdrew his licence to train.

It was an unhappy time for all connected with the Findon stable. Fred was not directly involved because Rosyth had been ridden in all his races by Josh Gifford, now the stable's second jockey, but the implications of the withdrawal of Ryan Price's licence were enormous. New homes had to be found for the 48 horses, stable lads and other employees had to find new jobs.

There was great uncertainty about it all, too, for the withdrawal of the licence was for an indefinite period, and though Ryan Price was told at the end of the enquiry that he could

apply for a licence for the following season at the end of
the current one, there was no certainty that the licence would
be granted.

It was this case that emphasised the problems which can
arise through the inability of the Stewards, under advice from
their lawyers, to issue a statement immediately after an
enquiry. The whole matter hinges on the fact that the Racing
Calendar has been established as a 'privileged' publication
and one in which the Stewards have the right to publish the
results of their enquiries.

The production of a press statement or any other device
which would publicise the result of an enquiry before its
publication in the Racing Calendar could involve them, or
any paper making use of the statement, in an action for
libel.

Thus the press are put in the unsatisfactory position of
having to rely on the owner, trainer or jockey who has
been the subject of the enquiry for a statement of what has
happened. Sometimes they refuse to say anything, sometimes they give the information only to a press man whom
they knew particularly well, and sometimes the information
even goes to the newspaper which is prepared to pay the
most for it. Sometimes there are inaccuracies, as in Ryan
Price's case.

When a man has just heard that his means of livelihood
is to be withdrawn, it is hardly surprising if his mind is in a
whirl. Ryan did not hear the Senior Steward, Lord Cadogan,
say that he could apply for a licence at the end of the season,
and he did not pass this information on to the press waiting
around the door of 12, Cavendish Square.

As a result, the Stewards were roundly attacked for not
putting a limit on the sentence. They had not, strictly, done
so, but a full statement would have lessened the verbal on-
slaught.

The most significant advance in the racing's public re-
lations in recent years has been the decision to issue, under

certain conditions, statements of local stewards' decisions taken at race meetings.

It still remains to clear up the unsatisfactory position about the results of enquiries by the Stewards of the Jockey Club and it is to be hoped that their legal advisers will find some formula which will enable the public to have a full statement immediately after the conclusion of these enquiries.

The disbanding of the Price stable went ahead rapidly. Some of the horses went to Ken Cundell, some to John Sutcliffe, others to Syd Dale and Harry Whiteman. Of the stable's two Grand National hopes, Out and About was put in the care of Ken Cundell, while Fred's mount Kilmore was sent to Epsom to be trained by Syd Dale, formerly Ryan Price's head lad.

Kilmore was Fred's only ride at Aintree this last season. He had been offered several rides in other races, but he was determined to avoid all possibility of injury, for he really thought that Kilmore could be the first 14-year-old ever to win Europe's toughest steeplechase. The going was soft, which was ideal for him, and Fred set out to ride in his last Grand National, following his now well-proven route and with complete confidence in his mount's ability to negotiate the 30 fences unprompted by him from the saddle.

Kilmore fell at the 21st fence just when Fred's hopes of ending his career with a Grand National victory were increasing with every stride :

He would have won – I swear he would have won. He was going easier than at any time in any of his three other Grand Nationals. We were just hack cantering, and to this day I don't know why he fell. It was the only time at Liverpool that he made a serious mistake of his own accord.

Aintree theorists would have had another setback if Kilmore *had* won at the age of 14. As it was, a 12-year-old,

Team Spirit, ridden by Willie Robinson, won the race, and at his fifth attempt. There are no rules governing Aintree. They are being re-made the whole time.

Fred had only three more rides before his final day at Cheltenham on April 11, and one winner, Vultrix, who won the Tote Investors Handicap Chase at Wolverhampton on March 25 comfortably. In the last few days, a small procession of journalists wended its way to Kitsbury to interview him and then pay tribute to him in print. As ever they found him courteous, frank, modest and with an ability to laugh at himself.

There was a big crowd at Cheltenham on that last day, and Fred desperately wanted to ride a winner to round off his career, but fate which had painted some colourful episodes during his career, failed on this occasion to produce the elements of drama and success for which everyone was hoping.

The nearest Fred came to riding a winner was in the Clive Graham Handicap Hurdle on this Beaverbrook Newspapers sponsored day. Peter O'Sullevan's Friendly Again was in the lead coming into the last hurdle but hard as Fred drove her up the hill, Owen McNally was going too well on Mishgar and beat him three lengths. 'Sorry it had to be us that beat you, Fred,' apologised Mishgar's trainer, Toby Balding.

Fred still had a ride on Kirriemuir in the *Evening Standard* Hurdle to which to look forward. Kirriemuir, owned by Diana's aunt, Mrs Doreen Beddington, had won his first seven races that season and had run a fine race for a four-year-old to finish third to Magic Court in the Champion Hurdle. The public made him an 11 to 10 on favourite.

Kirriemuir, however, did not sense the importance of the occasion. Perhaps feeling the effect of his Champion Hurdle effort, he was never going well. He jumped badly and finished last of the eight runners.

So it all rested on Sunbeat in the *Sunday Express* Handicap Chase over 4m. 1f. Sunbeat was right up with the leaders two fences from home, but then his stamina gave out and he finished only sixth – Fred's last ride in public.

Before Fred went out to ride Kirriemuir, the crowd flocked to the unsaddling enclosure as it had been announced that the Cheltenham Steeplechase Company would be making a presentation to him.

On behalf of the directors of the course on which Fred had ridden the winners of more than 60 races, including three Champion Hurdles and two Gold Cups, Lord Willoughby de Broke presented him with a silver cigarette box and asked him to accept honorary life membership of the Cheltenham Steeplechase Club.

There were other marks of the great affection that people in racing had for Fred. Mrs Max Aitken presented him with a silver statuette of a horse and rider on behalf of the day's sponsors, Beaverbrook Newspapers.

Three days later at the Savoy Hotel he was guest of honour at a 'Fred Winter Tribute Luncheon' given by the Variety Club of Great Britain.

It was one of the greatest gatherings of famous National Hunt riders there has ever been. The past National Hunt champion jockeys present included Gerry Wilson, 'Frenchie' Nicholson, Tim Molony, Dick Francis, Stan Mellor, Jack Dowdeswell, Bryan Marshall, Tim Brookshaw and Fred Rimell, while riders of Grand National winners who came to honour Fred were Pat Taaffe, Fulke Walwyn, Captain Bobby Petre, Arthur Freeman, Michael Scudamore, Tim Hamey, Gerry Scott, Bobby Beasley, Johnny Bullock, Leo McMorrow, Dave Dick, Jimmy Power and Pat Buckley.

There were many tributes paid to Fred in the speeches after lunch. The Queen Mother's trainer, Peter Cazalet, said 'Thank you Fred Winter, for your splendid example to all the young jockeys. Few individuals stand out in leadership as you do, and during the last 10 years you have stood out alone.'

Clive Graham, who compered the occasion, read a telegram from American trainer Pete Bostwick: 'Please congratulate Fred on a record that was a great credit to the jumping game. Those of us who saw him have happiest recollections of his fine ride on Baby Prince at Belmont Park. Please express to him our very best wishes for continued success in his new career.'

A sobering note was the presence in a wheelchair of Tim Brookshaw, paralysed below the waist since his fall 14 months earlier. Not every steeplechase jockey's career ends on a happy note.

During the luncheon, Fred received from the Variety Club a cheque for £600 towards the fund for the children of Tim Brookshaw and for Paddy Farrell, who sustained similar but even more serious injuries when Border Flight fell in the 1964 Grand National.

For Fred, the most daunting moment of the occasion was standing up to reply to all the tributes, but his performance was typical. He thanked all those who had made his success possible – his wife Diana, his father and mother, Ryan Price, his doctor and physiotherapist, and many others. 'But these aren't all. There are the gatemen at courses all over the country and all those newspaper sellers who can make your day with a grin and a cheery "good morning". These are the people, *all* of them, who have given me my career. Thank you.'

At the end of Fred's riding career, Ryan Price said that he would himself never have been where he was (at the top of his profession as a National Hunt trainer) if it had not been for Fred. It is a measure of the success and loyalty of the partnership over so many years that Fred, too, felt a debt of gratitude to Ryan Price and believes that he would not have had anything like the success he did have if it had not been for Ryan's support.

This was one of racing's truly great teams, and, for Ryan, Fred's retirement was a sad moment:

'I wish Fred could have gone on riding for ever and ever.

I didn't want it to finish. Never mind what Fred says – at the end he was giving a horse as good a ride as at any stage of his career.

'Yet, you know, he had an inferiority complex and never had real faith in his own remarkable ability. He always thought there were three or four in a race that would go better than him. But he rode me at least a hundred winners that no one else in the world would have won on. He was an inspired man – a genius. It will be a very long time before we see his equal.

'When he retired he was just the same person as when he started. He never altered one iota. We never had a written contract for the last ten years. At the start of the season he would say "Ryan, same as last year?". In the last few years he could have had three or four times the retainer he was getting from my stable if he had taken up some of the offers that were made to him, but he stayed with me.

'He was the most useless schooling jockey this world has ever produced, but once he was engaged in a race, every-thing clicked into place. Most jockeys don't worry about what makes a particular horse tick. They just get on them and give them a kick in the belly. But Fred wanted to learn about each horse. He wanted to find the key to them all.

'He was mad keen on statistics, and always wanted to ride a higher average of winners than anyone else. After getting beat on a horse, that night at dinner he would go over the race, every inch of the way, saying "If I had done this or this, he would nearly have won".

'After a time, one began to realise that this was a *jockey*, and you had to let him do what he wanted in a race. We had our rows, such as when he went to the front too soon on Clair Soleil in the Champion, and when he was beaten on Cortego at Liverpool. But that day it was bad psychology on my part, laying a horse out for a gamble when it would be Fred's first ride on National day. He *had* to be thinking about the National. Still, I was very, very angry. I told him

141

we had kids in the yard who could have ridden a better race than he did.

'Then he went out on Sundew and won, and as he was riding back he saw me in the crowd. He just grinned and stuck two fingers in the air.

'Usually I allowed him tremendous liberty and didn't tie him down with orders. In fact, I got a rocket for it once. The Stewards called me in at Newbury and asked me what orders I had given Fred in a particular race. They were horrified when I said I hadn't given him any orders. I mean, what orders would you give Lester Piggott?

'Perhaps the thing that sums up Fred's attitude to dishonesty in racing is what happened when an owner said to him in the paddock one day "I don't want you to be in the first three in this race". Fred narrowed his eyes and looked at him very hard and said "Listen, you had better go and back this horse, because it is going to *win*'." And it did.

'Very few people realise what a great character this person was. He raised the standard of National Hunt jockeyship higher than it has ever been, and I don't mean just by his riding, but by his conduct both on and off the course. I'm sorry it had to come to an end.'

CHAPTER TWELVE

WE NEVER KNEW WHAT
HARD WORK WAS

Once Fred had taken the decision to become a trainer, he and Diana started to look for a suitable training establishment, and during the last eight months of his riding career they visited a number of possible stables in Berkshire.

They were sad that they would have to leave their charming home near Stow-on-the-Wold, for they had many friends in the district, but there were no training facilities there. Fred wanted if possible to find a place in Lambourn as it was the only training centre that he knew really well, and he knew many of the people who lived and worked there.

In August 1963, they drove over to Lambourn to look at Uplands, the stables which became vacant when Charlie Pratt and his wife were killed flying back one stormy Saturday from Redcar after winning the William Hill Gold Cup with Songedor. They liked the house, nestling under a ridge of the downs and with a convenient lane leading up to the gallops.

It was to be put up for auction, but the sale was too soon for them. Fred could not afford to buy the place and have it lying idle for some eight months. At the auction, Uplands was bought by Doug Marks, who until then had been training at Winkfield Row, near Ascot.

The search went on. Fred and Diana looked at more stables and by Christmas they were regretting even more that they had not been able to buy Uplands when it was on the market. Fred met Doug Marks at the races one day and more jokingly than with any real hope, asked him if he would take a profit on Uplands.

The trainer laughed and shook his head, but to Fred's surprise and delight, a few days later when they met at the races, Doug Marks said he could have the place. He had decided to look for somewhere with a smaller house.

Immediately Fred announced in November that he was retiring, Mr Michael Sobell, for whom he used to ride Flame Gun, wrote to him saying that he would be very glad if Fred would train a couple of horses for Mrs Sobell. By Christmas Day, Solbina and One Seven Seven, two horses which Mr Sobell bought in Ireland had arrived at Kitsbury and went into the paddock there. They were joined by Royal Sanction, whom Fred's father used to train for Mr Cyril Walkling. This was the nucleus of the Winter stable.

Besides horses, Fred needed good stable staff. He realised that while he was riding he had never really taken a great deal of interest in stable routine and all the ins and outs of training. He was fortunate in being able to assemble an excellent team.

An early recruit was Brian Delaney, who used to ride for Fred's neighbour in Gloucestershire, Hector Smith, and has recently became Fred's head lad.

Richard Pitman, who had been with John Roberts at Cheltenham and had ridden a number of winners, also joined the new stable with the promise of a few rides.

Fred was also faced with the problem of finding a stable jockey. He chose Eddie Harty, the pipe-smoking Irishman from a huge family, a number of whom have made a name for themselves in the saddle. Eddie had been riding as an amateur, but had now graduated to professional. His style of riding was so different to Fred's own that one wondered how Fred had chosen him:

The main reason that I respect him is that he is a horseman. I have never thought of myself as a real horseman in any way. Jockeyship can be learned. Eddie is not stylish, but style is not what counts. If you are stylish you can look very good and still get beat a neck. I remember Eddie won a short head on Fool's Delight at Sandown one day, and it would not have been a disgrace to Lester Piggott.

Fred was asked to take four horses from Findon, after Ryan Price lost his licence. They were Anglo and Mousquet, both owned by Mr Stuart Levy, and Mr Nat Cohen's Quintina and Master Andrew.

In July the Winter family moved from Kitsbury Orchard to Uplands, Lambourn, bringing with them ponies, dogs, hunters, children, and Solbina, One Seven Seven and Royal Sanction.

The four horses arrived from Findon. With seven horses, and several more promised to him by owners for whom he had ridden in the past, Fred was in business as a trainer.

Di and I never knew what hard work was until I started training. As a jockey, you have to watch your weight, of course, and there's the odd bit of schooling and riding gallops. You get your Calendar and mark your rides off at the beginning of the week. You drive to the course and ride them, and that's the end of your responsibility. With training, you really have to use your brain the whole time, dealing with people as well as horses, doing the entries, buying hay, entertaining owners and keeping them informed about their horses, worrying about staff, finding new horses. And the telephone. It never stops.

One phone call which came before the Winters had left Kitsbury was to play a vital part in Fred's first season as a trainer. It was from Tommy Smith, the young rider and trainer of Jay Trump, twice the winner of the Maryland Hunt Cup and one of the best jumpers of the solid American timber fences that had ever been seen.

F   145

Tommy Smith was seeking advice. He and Jay Trump's owner, Mrs Mary Stephenson, had decided that, if it was at all possible. Jay Trump should be allowed to prove his ability in the English Grand National. No horse had ever won both the Maryland Hunt Cup and the Grand National, though Billy Barton in 1922 had gone close, falling at the last fence at Aintree when he had every chance of winning, and then being remounted to finish second to the only other to survive the course, Tipperary Tim.

The odds against Jay Trump bringing off the double were enormous, but those of the American hunt racing community who knew of the plan were tremendously excited at the idea of their local champion crossing the Atlantic to tackle the huge fences at Aintree.

Before anything could happen, Jay Trump's connections needed to know a lot more about English steeplechasing and the Grand National conditions in particular.

What follows is not a conversation. It is what the two men most concerned with Jay Trump's eventual triumph at Aintree told the writer at different times about the events leading up to the race and what happened in the race itself – how two men of completely different character and temperament came to form a team dedicated to one aim – victory in the Grand National with Jay Trump:

Tommy Smith: I had discussed with Mrs Stephenson all the problems and technicalities of British racing, and getting her horse qualified for the Grand National. Her father gave me Fred Winter's phone number and suggested I should ask him just what was involved. I tried to call him and it took about two days to get through to Kitsbury. When I did get through, I told Fred about Jay Trump and that I wanted to run him in the National, and what were the conditions. He outlined them to me and pointed out I would have to get Jay Trump qualified with three races before January 6 if he was going to be properly handicapped. Then Fred said where are you going to send him, and I said I had hoped a cousin of mine, Dan Moore, would train him in Ireland and I asked Fred what he thought of this plan. When I asked him that, I was not really aware that Fred was a trainer himself. You know, the last we heard of him he was a jockey and still riding. Fred said I don't think you would do best if the horse was sent over to Ireland. In the first place you have to get him qualified and you would have a hard job doing that because the value of the races in Ireland is lower than in England. Also, your horse will want the top of the ground, which you won't find in Ireland very often. So I said what should I do and Fred said well you could send the horse to me. I've just started training, and of course if you send the horse to me you will get more individual attention than if you go to a large public trainer, because I haven't got many horses. So that's what I did.

Tommy had just married Frances Cochran and they were actually on their honeymoon when they came over and stayed at the Red Lion in Lambourn. There's nothing wrong with the Red Lion, but it hasn't got all the mod. cons. that an American young lady would be used to and I think Frances was pretty miserable for her first few weeks in England. Later on she loved it. Then Tommy went back alone to America to fetch the horse and there was a delay because the box the airline had produced was not long enough for the horse, and Frances was stuck in Lambourn by herself for three days while they rebuilt the stall — you know, this was right at the start of her honeymoon. Anyway Tommy and Jay Trump got here safely in the end, and we were able to have a good look at this horse, who'd won a couple of Maryland Hunt Cups. He wasn't what you would call a typical English racehorse, but he was a lovely horse — terrific power, great bone, very well balanced, great outlook, a great big honest head.

Tommy: Jay Trump's dam cost 50 dollars, and I bought the horse himself for 2,000 dollars for Mrs Stephenson with the aim of winning a Maryland Hunt Cup. After he'd been gelded, Bobby Fenwick used to hunt him with the Green Spring Hounds. He was one of the hunt staff horses. He was temperamental to start with but that first year, as a four-year-old, he was Grand Champion at the Elkridge – Harford hunter trials.

This horse was brilliant. He would do dressage, three-day event courses, fox-hunting. I had instilled it in him to jump every type of obstacle when he was three and four years old. He had never fallen anywhere. A couple of times I thought we had had it, but somehow he would get out of trouble. In a schooling ring you couldn't make him do anything wrong.

I was pre-warned about Tommy – that he was rather difficult to deal with and very self-opinionated, had his own ideas. So when he first came over, I must admit that I rather had my back up before we even met. Then the yard was in a complete shambles, we had only just moved in. I had about eight or ten horses by then. I said we would go out at 7.30 a.m. the first morning he was there to ride out.
That morning, by the time he arrived, we had been walking round the yard two or three minutes, all mounted, and I said, Mr Smith, when we say 7.30 we mean 7.30 and not 7.35. We put him up on Anglo, the first horse he ever sat on in England, and within a few seconds he was on his backside.

Tommy: In retrospect, my first day with Fred was hilarious, though it wasn't funny at the time. In the States, I used to ride for myself, and I used to go out and do a bit of work with Jay Trump just when I felt like it. No really set routine. Well, this first morning, I misjudged the time it would take me to walk from the Red Lion to Fred's yard, and I was about five minutes late.

They were all saddled and mounted and walking round

the yard, and Fred looked very grim. I went over to this animal, which actually was the Grand National winner of the following season, and just before the lad threw me up in the saddle he said you must watch this one, he's a bit fresh. He threw me up, and of course in America they usually walk you round a couple of turns while you get settled before they let go the rein. I was not on the horse more than three seconds, before Anglo put his head down and gave a good buck, and I was mortified to find myself lying there in the yard with all the lads grinning. The lad who had put me up looked down at me and said 'Well, I would never have known you were an amateur until I saw you ride.' To finish it off, about five minutes later when I'm back on the horse and we are going up the track from Fred's yard to the gallops, I pull out a cigarette to calm my nerves, and a voice from behind me says Mr Smith, when we ride, we don't smoke.

He is, in fact, a very intelligent young man. He had been training Jay Trump for several years, and he went into this Grand National business in typical American fashion. He analyses everything, and everything he does there's got to be a reason for it. He studied the horse's diet in detail. Everything we fed him, he would say what is it? He thought the oats were OK but he was very critical of the hay. We had a fair few discussions but everything went on all right.

Tommy: I had my own ideas about the horse because I had been with him for five years, but by the same token I didn't know anything about English racing and the conditions the horse would be subjected to, or the feeding and so on. I had to rely on Fred to be the trainer, there is no question about that, and he had to rely on me for information about the horse. On the whole it was a coalition. He had his part and I had mine, and as it turned out we complemented each other, but Fred was always the boss. I was the rider.

He had had a lot of experience in timber and brush races in the States. If a man has formed a style, you should not try to alter it. He was intelligent, and, as we went on, very courageous. The only criticism was that he would ride on the point of his toe, which is both ugly and impracticable. I had to get on to him time and again about this.

Tommy: That Fall, the ground was very hard and they were even cancelling meetings because of the hard ground, which I'd never heard of. I was walking round saying this is the best going I have ever seen, and all we were doing was trotting around on the roads. We hadn't even had a good work out.

We got the horses going in the usual English way with plenty of road work, which they never do in the States. They just don't think road work is good for them. Then when we started trotting on long hills on the road, Tommy wanted to know why we couldn't trot on the grass. Then we did some cantering on the dirt track because the grass was so hard. Tommy kept saying I must school him, I must school him, so in the end one day when we were trotting on Mandown I let him jump a couple of hurdles. The ground was like iron.

Tommy: I said, this going won't bother this horse. They have these little miniature hurdles, and I cantered Jay Trump up to them like a pony in a show ring, and he popped over them. Then I wanted to jump something bigger, so we went over a couple of the steeplechase fences. I said, this is child's play. Fred said that will do.

It was the most extraordinary performance I have ever seen. You know what we are in this game – it's all a gradual process. Tommy took this horse who was a complete stranger – mind you they are not big fences, but they were the first

150

English ones he'd seen and they are a bit black and not very inviting – and he sailed over them.

It got towards the middle of October, and we had him entered at Sandown on October 21 and he still hadn't done any real work. We decided he had just got to do some work on a racecourse, so I phoned Frank Osgood, the manager at Newbury racecourse, and got permission to work there. I rode Mousquet, Tommy was on Jay Trump and Richard Pitman rode One Seven Seven, and we worked from the seven furlongs gate. I told Tommy to stay behind us and come up to us in the last furlong. One of us knocked into Jay Trump on the turn into the straight, which wasn't very clever, and I thought that's the end of him, but inside the last furlong he came past us as if we were standing still. This was the first intimation I had that he was a decent sort of horse.

Tommy: At Sandown, I think, Fred had still no real clue as to what sort of a horse he had in Jay Trump. I never asked him how he thought the horse was going to run. He told me I ought to try to let him go along in touch with the leaders, three or four lengths behind, and let him get the feel of racing over British fences, but not to worry if he lost ground and not to push him. If he seemed to like what was happening, Fred said, then you might think about doing something after the three quick fences down by the station, but if he doesn't seem to get the knack of it, then wait for another day.

He was a bit sticky over the first four fences, but after that he was brilliant. Everything went smoothly. Tommy did everything I told him, and he came there between the last two and beat the favourite, Comforting Wave, by five lengths. They were not a very good field, but it was a surprise. He was my first winner.

151

Tommy: After we had won, I was slightly surprised by the tremendous crowd round the unsaddling enclosure, all cheering. Then I suddenly realised they were cheering because it was Fred's first winner.

* * *

Jay Trump next won a three miles 'chase at Windsor a month after the Sandown Park race ('not impressive' said the form book), was beaten ten lengths as the only contestant against Frenchman's Cove in the King George VI Chase at Kempton Park on Boxing Day, won a three miles 'chase for amateurs at Newbury on February 19, and was only fifth to Meon Valley in the Royal Porcelain Handicap Chase at Worcester, just 10 days before the Grand National.

* * *

I was terrified because Tommy had had only four or five rides in England, and always on the same horse. He would not ride any other horses, though he was offered a number of rides. This was when one began to have doubts about his courage, and I remember a day at Windsor when he saw seven or eight falls and made some remark which sort of strengthened one's suspicions. But in fact he had got more guts in refusing to take other rides. He said I have come here for one reason, to win the Grand National, and I'm not going to take a chance until I have fulfilled that.

Tommy: I have never worked with anyone in my life who could instil you with so much confidence by being so helpful and determined. He at least appeared to be confident that the job was going to be done properly. He had a marvellous understanding of what a rider is feeling in the paddock as he gets up to go out. We would have worked it all out the night before a race and Fred would be relaxed in the paddock and would never say any more about the contest or give any more instructions. He knows last-minute advice can be unnerving, and he would just give you a leg up and say 'Have a good time, God bless'. Mind you, if you did something he didn't like, he didn't wait until tomorrow to tell you.

Tommy made great friends with Keith Piggott, who has a film projector, and we spent a great deal of time looking at the National films, over and over again. I could only teach him what I thought was the right way round. We used to talk things over. I would point out where I was at any time in the race. He soaked it all in.

Tommy: When we got nearer the National, it all became much more intensive, this conditioning of rider Smith. Day after day we went over and over in slow motion old Grand National films from the last five years. Fred would point out people doing things right or making mistakes. Most English horses tend to jump to the outside, but Fred said watch Beasley on Nicolaus Silver. He was brilliant. He said notice that at every fence with the exception maybe of the Chair there is always room for three to four horses on the inside. The inside drop is worse and the fences are stiffer, but your horse is either going to jump it or he isn't, so it is far better to go round by the quieter route. He showed me his ride on Sundew when he fell and said this is the way *not* to do it. We used to go over and over the Canal Turn. Fred would say when you get to the 23rd get into a good position, move out from the rails so you jump the Canal Turn at 45 degrees. Beasley did it brilliantly on Nicolaus Silver. He would say, they will go a terrific gallop the first mile. This is because they are mad. You get your horse in a nice comfortable pace – just sit there and hunt. The object of the game is to get round. Don't ask him to stand off any of the fences. I used to say I will never make it, but Fred always managed to minimise the tension somehow. It's a fact that very few great people, particularly sportsmen, are articulate and very few of them know why they do what they do. We all know that Fred is a great rider, but he is also a great teacher, and he makes you understand what you've got to do and why.

153

As soon as the coughing broke out, and it was really bad that year, I put Jay Trump in some seperate boxes out at the back of the stables, with Solbina for company. I was going round the yard twice a day to see the patients. It took about ten days for a horse to lose the cough, and they were left very weak afterwards. The whole thing went on for about a month. Every horse in the yard except Jay Trump coughed, including Solbina. Tommy found a place opposite his cottage, four boxes practically new, built by Lady Ann FitzAlan-Howard. They hadn't been used for a couple of years. We put Jay Trump in there and Tommy looked after the horse entirely. No one else set foot in the place, except me. I used to go down each morning and evening, and stand in a tray of disinfectant. If Tommy gave the thumbs up sign, I wouldn't go near him. He used to go up the gallops by himself. On work mornings we used to rustle up what we could to do a gallop with Jay Trump. I think it is just possible he did have a slight touch of the virus, even though he did not cough. He looked awful and he ran that disappointing race at Worcester.

*　　*　　*

All this was being recorded by a B.B.C. camera unit making the film called *The Favourites*, directed by Anthony de Lotbiniere. Two horses had been chosen as the principal actors in this film which would depict the preparations for the great race at Aintree, and the race itself. The two were Jay Trump and the Scottish horse Freddie, and incredibly for the film makers these two finished first and second. It was a film which captured more of the feeling of National Hunt racing and the Grand National than any other before or since.

The camera team covering Jay Trump's preparation camped out at Lambourn, followed the American horse to Worcester for that disheartening race 10 days before the National, filmed Jay Trump's departure for Aintree 48 hours before the big race, and Tommy Smith and Fred Winter

154

setting out on foot round the course to look at those daunting fences from ground level, where they look even more frightening than they do from the back of a horse.

*   *   *

Tommy had seen all the films now and it was really the day before the race that we crystallised the plan. We walked round the course, stopping at every fence, and I showed him where I would like him to go and where he should be at any given time. In the actual race it was marvellous to see him the first time round passing the stands just where you wanted him to be and following the route you had both planned.

Tommy: I had spent so much time with Fred and we had gone over it so much that it was as if I was not really riding that horse. Fred had impressed himself so much on my personality, it was as if the whole thing was detached and separate from me and as if he rode in the race himself. I just watched it all happen. I know it sounds fanciful, but I suppose it happens in other walks of life – with a ballet master or a conductor of an orchestra, or someone like that, but it was uncanny. I don't really believe in telepathy, but when Fred was shouting at me to put that whip down and I did – well that's as near as you'll get to telepathy.

Tommy rode him exactly as I told him to ride. He followed the route exactly and everything I told him. I thought perhaps he had come to the front a little sooner than I wanted him to, but I thought he was a certainty coming to the last. Then he went two lengths in front after the last, and when he came to the elbow he had his stick up on the left side. He pulled it through to the right, which was perfect, but then he started to hit him. I shouted No, No, put it down. Jay Trump hated being hit and his tail was beginning to go round. Then Tommy put his whip down and the horse ran on. The last 200 yards were agony, sheer agony. But he won.

CHAPTER THIRTEEN

JAY TRUMP GOES TO FRANCE

Fred was to experience again a few weeks later the agony of watching Jay Trump, the first good horse he ever trained, involved in a close finish for an important race, but this time not with such a happy result as at Aintree.

Jay Trump returned to Lambourn in triumph, and plans were soon being made for him to go to France for the Grand Steeplechase de Paris. What a superb treble it would be to complete – the Maryland Hunt Cup, the Grand National and the Grand Steeplechase de Paris.

Never before, and perhaps never again, could a horse have been in a position to achieve victory in the three hardest steeplechases in the world within 15 months.

A fortnight after the Grand National, Jay Trump was obviously feeling as good as he had ever felt. He had come through the race without a scratch on him. If there was ever a year for him to tackle the French race, this was it.

Late in May, Jay Trump left Fred's yard, never to return again. He was flown from London Airport to Le Bourget and then driven to Chantilly, where he was lodged in the yard of ex-steeplechase jockey Paul Peraldi.

With four weeks to go to the big race, Fred moved into the Hotel du Parc in Chantilly with Tommy and Frances, and the business began of teaching Jay Trump to forget all about Aintree's massive fences and learn instead to jump the varied French obstacles with the fluency that was so essential if he was not to lose lengths to his experienced rivals at every fence.

On June 10, ten days before the Grand Steeplechase,

Jay Trump ran in a 2¾m. 'chase over part of the big race course at Auteuil. Apart from jumping the bullfinch and the big, 5 ft 9 ins hedge rather slowly, he did not put a foot wrong and ran an excellent race to finish fourth, beaten about ten lengths.

Fred was satisfied that Jay Trump was well enough to give a good account of himself in the big race. Tommy's pride in his mount's versatility had again been justified. In May the previous year, he had been jumping solid timber fences in Maryland. He had quickly discovered the knack of clearing English brush fences when he had made his first appearance at Sandown Park in November, and now he had shown that the completely different technique required for French jumps held no problems for him.

Jay Trump's win at Aintree drew in his wake a mass of English and American jumping fans to Auteuil on the day that he set out round the devious course that Fred had covered two years earlier on Mandarin.

Tommy had been faced with the problem of shedding 16 lb so that he could ride at 10 st 1 lb. He went about it with his usual dedication, spending long hours in a Paris gymnasium doing exercises while wearing a rubber sweat suit. He ate little breakfast, 'Metrecal' for lunch, steak for dinner. The pounds rolled off.

The day of the big race, the temperature was in the 70's. Tommy weighed out at 10 st 1 lb, and went out on Jay Trump hard, fit, taught and tense, lighter than he had ever been since he was in his teens.

In Fred's view, his wasting probably cost him the race.

Jay Trump was among the first four or five the whole way. He jumped well, but again at the bullfinch he lost ground. His leap at the big water jump was so huge that he pecked slightly on landing, but at almost every fence he gained ground in the air.

With three-quarters of a mile to go, Jay Trump was just in the lead and full of running. At this point there were those

157

in the stands who thought Tommy should have kicked on and let the others catch him if they could.

Jay Trump did not have much finishing speed, but he did stay for ever. If he dallied with the others now, there would surely be something which would outrun him from the last fence.

But clouding the issue in Tommy's mind were his worries about the bullfinch, which had to be jumped yet again – the second last fence. If Jay Trump had no other horse to keep him company, he might prop and lose many lengths at this jump. Tommy decided to stay with the leaders.

Round the last bend, with just the bullfinch and a plain fence to jump, Tommy swung out slightly to let another horse come up on the inside so that he would jump the bullfinch alongside Jay Trump. They rose it together and this time Jay Trump handled the jump perfectly. He gained ground and was in front when he landed over the final fence.

But on the flat it was a different story. Hyeres III, the previous year's winner, and Yasco had too much speed for Jay Trump. He was third, beaten a length and three-quarters.

I think Tommy was too dedicated, too tightened up. He had got down to a ridiculous weight for someone of his build, and because of the wasting, I don't think he was capable of thinking clearly. If he had kicked on when he took up the running, they would never have caught him. I know Tommy felt the same afterwards. Then he didn't ride a finish at all. He could hardly move on the horse. He was too dried up.

Even so, it was a fine effort to come so tantalisingly close to landing a great international steeplechasing treble.

Fred and Diana saw Jay Trump run just once more before this great horse was retired. In April, 1966, they flew to America and saw Tommy win the Maryland Hunt Cup for the third time, easily beating Mountain Dew, who had also won the race twice.

By this time the Fred Winter story had taken another leap forward with an incredible second victory in the Grand National in only his second season as a trainer.

Anglo, a little, bright chestnut with a lot of white on his face, gave Fred his fourth Grand National triumph – two as a jockey and two as a trainer. He had ridden Anglo himself on several occasions in his last two seasons as a jockey, and won a long distance hurdle on him at Worcester, wearing the colours that Kilmore had carried in the Grand National.

Anglo came to Fred when Ryan Price's licence was withdrawn. He had graduated to jumping fences during the 1964–65 season while still with Ryan, and had won a sequence of novice 'chases. With Fred he was placed three times before Christmas in the 1965–66 season.

Fred decided to sharpen him up with an outing over hurdles at Ascot on December 16, but Anglo ran badly and sulked the whole way round. Fred sent him back to Windsor the next day, and this time he won a three miles 'chase comfortably. The opposition was not strong.

I never dreamed Anglo would win the National, though we had roughly planned his season with the race in mind. To start with, you would never expect to win the race two years running, and secondly, on a park course, he was nothing more than a moderate three miles chaser. All he needed was a distance of ground. Early in the season I did say to his owners he's not the best jumper in the world but with a bit more experience he might make a Grand National horse.
Eddie Harty broke his thigh in November, so I got Tim Norman to ride him. Tim got on with him very well, and they had great confidence in each other. From being a slightly chancy jumper, Anglo became very safe. In his race before the Grand National, he ran quite well at Kempton, which was not an ideal course for him, and finished fourth

159

to Kapeno, who was one of the first half dozen in the betting on the National. I must say that I thought Anglo was all of a 50 to 1 chance, which is the price he started at.

With Tim Norman, it was exactly the same as it had been with Tommy Smith. We showed him all the old National films. I told him where to go and what to do, and it worked like a dream. He hunted round, keeping out of trouble in the same way Tommy had done. He went to the front two from home. He beat Freddie 20 lengths. It was almost embarrassing standing in that winner's enclosure again, when you think of all the people who have been training horses for years and always had the luck go against them at Aintree.

Sadly, Anglo's form deteriorated after that. On a day at Worcester in March 1967 when the distance was 3m. 5f. and the going was heavy, he came into his own again briefly and won for Mr John R. Gaines, an American who had purchased him during the summer of 1966, but in the National he trailed behind from the start and was pulled up before he had completed a circuit.

He earned himself something of a reputation as a 'dog', and in five races during the 1967–68 season he was placed once, at Lingfield Park in February. Soon after that he began to lose his condition and his appetite. He picked up for a while, and then began to deteriorate rapidly.

Eventually, it was decided that Anglo would have to be put down. The post-mortem showed that he had a ruptured heart, and it was amazing that he had stayed alive so long.

Horses cannot tell you what is wrong with them and what is hurting them. The life of the vet and the trainer would be so much easier if they could. Many horses branded as ungenerous as Anglo was towards the end of his career, may have very good reasons apart from sheer laziness for not wanting to gallop flat out. The man who can put his finger on the trouble without being able to cross-examine the patient is worth his weight in gold.

CHAPTER FOURTEEN

THE STORY GOES ON

The Fred Winter story is, of course, unfinished. For ten months of the year Fred does the daily round of the jumping courses he came to know so well as a jockey: anywhere that there's a race to be won.

In his first four seasons as a trainer he saddled 131 winners and thought the total ought to have been larger:

I think I made a lot of mistakes through hurrying too much. All owners want quick results, but some horses want much more time than you realise. If you buy an unbroken three-year-old, he is going to need at least 18 months before he is a racehorse, sometimes much more. The easiest horse to train is one that has just come from flat racing. He knows how to use himself as a racehorse. All you have to do is to teach him to jump.

Fred rides out every morning. He is only three or four pounds heavier than when he was a jockey. Sometimes he schools a horse over hurdles or rides in a gallop to get a close view of a horse he is preparing for a big race. More often he goes out on one of the string who may not be doing serious work, which enables him to wait at the end of the gallops and watch the others do their work.

Often during school holidays, a small string of the Winter daughters on ponies, dwarfed by the racehorses, goes out with the second lot.

If you arrive at Uplands about midday for lunch, the second lot are usually just coming back, slip-slopping down the hill into the yard, past the end box from which Anglo, with white face and flaxen mane, used to watch all the activity, nodding his head hopefully at anyone who might conceivably come over and give him a peppermint. A terrier stands outside the house, tail-stump wagging idly as the horses come in.

Fred hands out king-size gin and tonics in the lounge with its paintings of Jay Trump, Sundew, and one of Clair Soleil by Madeleine Selfe, given to Fred by his brother John.

Fred sits down in slightly tatty jodhpurs to look at the runners for tomorrow marked off for him in the *Sporting Life* by the stable's secretary, Lawrence Eliot. It is the sign for the telephone to ring for about the twentieth time this morning.

No, I haven't had a chance to look at the book yet. Listen you're a better judge of form than I am. All I can say is, your horse is very, very well indeed, and if you think he's got a chance on the book, then he'll take a lot of beating. See you there tomorrow, I shan't arrive till about the second race. Got to go and look at a horse at Epsom first.

Fred puts down the phone.

Come on, let's go and eat. You won't mind lunching in the kitchen. Bring your drink with you ... Have some potatoes. Yes, well, you could afford to lose a bit of weight. Di, make her use her fork properly, she look's as though she's mucking out a box. Lawrence, did you phone Weatherby's about those colours. That horse runs tomorrow.
Listen, your pony looked definitely rough when you came out with us this morning. It would be a good idea if you all tried a bit harder if you're going to ride out in the mornings.

'Mummy, do you know, Sister Josephine *always* listens to the racing results on the wireless every evening.'

162

'I hope you didn't tell her to back Peralto the other day.'

'Well, I don't know if she actually *backs* horses. But she *does* listen to the results.'

'Mr Hedges, what are you going to put in this book about Daddy. Will it have pictures of the Grand National and all that.'

'Daddy rode in the Grand National nine times. And he won it twice. And we've won it twice since we came to live here.'

'Pass the gravy please, and get on with your lunch. You're talking too much.'

The End
– for the moment, anyway.

FOR THE RECORD

Fred Winter rode in 4,284 races in England. He won 923 of them, was second 577 times, third 509 times, and fell 319 times.

Season by Season

His riding record in England:

	Rides	1st	2nd	3rd	Falls
1947–48	9	2	0	0	1
1948–49	3	1	0	0	1
1949–50	131	18	20	13	14
1950–51	221	38	28	29	18
1951–52	404	85	53	50	29
1952–53	470	121	74	71	41
1953–54	1	0	0	0	1
1954–55	324	65	51	39	28
1955–56	344	74	50	51	23
1956–57	323	80	48	42	21
1957–58	359	82	38	43	17
1958–59	307	74	31	24	33
1959–60	341	67	48	32	29
1960–61	383	82	51	49	22
1961–62	311	62	45	35	21
1962–63	181	29	18	18	7
1963–64	172	43	22	13	13
Total	4,284	923	577	509	319

His record abroad was :

1961–62

France	5	3	0	0	0
1962–63					
Ireland	3	1	0	0	0
France	2	0	0	0	0
U.S.A.	2	1	0	0	0
1963–64					
Ireland	2	1	0	0	0
Grand total	4,298	929	577	509	319

INDEX

167

Winter, Mrs Fred sr, 14, 16, 23, 52, 140

Winter, Joanna, 69, 72–3, 88, 108, 124, 161

Winter, John, 9–10, 14–16, 69, 79, 162

Winter, Pat, *see* Smith, Pat

Winter, Philippa, 69, 81, 88, 108, 124, 161

Winter, Sheila, 15

Withington, Fred, 41

Wragg, Harry, 17

Wyndburgh, 76, 96, 104

Xanthor, 108

Yasco, 158